Join A Housing Co-op What Could Go Wrong?

A True Story of Bullying, Betrayal -
and the Fight to Stay Sane in a System that was
Supposed to Protect You

Mark Linden OMeara

© 2025 Mark Linden O'Meara

All rights reserved. This book, or any parts thereof, may not be reproduced or transmitted in any manner whatsoever, transmitted electronically, or distributed by any means without the written permission of the publisher.

Why I Wrote This Story

This story is based on my lived experience in a housing co-operative. I never imagined that what was marketed as a model of community living would turn into a prolonged ordeal of bullying, harassment, and systemic negligence. I wrote this not out of bitterness, but from a desire for truth, healing, and reform.

For years, I tried every reasonable method to resolve maintenance issues specific to my unit (my unit was directly above the electrical room, boiler room, and elevator mechanical room), address safety hazards, and raise concerns through appropriate channels — including internal grievance processes, mediation, formal work orders, and legal action. Instead of resolution, I faced retaliation, dismissal, termination, threats of physical harm, verbal abuse, behavior towards me that could be considered criminal harassment, gaslighting and further psychological harm.

I documented my journey not only to process the trauma I endured, but also to highlight broader issues that can — and do — occur in co-operative housing when accountability is absent and governance is manipulated.

While names and identifying details have been changed to protect privacy, the events are presented truthfully and based on evidence. This narrative is not an attack on individuals, but a call for better oversight, protections for vulnerable residents, and reform of the systems meant to serve and safeguard tenants.

I have tried my best to order the events chronologically based on my documentation and records.

I hope this account helps others feel less alone, encourages dialogue, and prompts real change.

— Mark Linden O'Meara

Table of Contents

The Offer 1
Minimal Elevator Noise 3
Joining the Maintenance Committee 3
David and William – History of Maintenance 4
Conflict Starts 6
The Reputation Attacking Begins 8
Reconciliation? 8
Scrutiny of Finances and Maintenance. 9
The Co-op Tractor 11
An Elevator from Hell 11
Master Keys and Store Accounts 12
Wasting Road Salt 13
Fast Forward to Next Summer: 14
Fixing a Camera Leads to Removal 15
Noisy Garage Fan Conflict 16
The Whir, Whir, Whir Fan 18
News Breaks 19
Flooded Unit 19
Bang Bang—It's not the Compressor. 19
Fix a Leak -Accused of Making a Mess 22
Front Lawn Destruction 22
David Riles Up My Neigbour 23
Bang, Bang, Bang Part III 24

Garage Door Comes Down on a Guy's Vehicle	25
Bang, Bang, Bang continued.	26
Garage Leak Repairs – Are we Being Hosed?	26
The AGM – No Elections	27
Roger Moves - Can't Close Financing.	27
More Bullying to a Different Member	28
Elevator Noise Starts to Get Bothersome	28
Meetings and Mediators	28
Andy's Harassment and Attempted Eviction	29
Shrubs Cut Again	29
Neighbor Floods Her Apartment	30
Saving The Tree	31
Building Envelop and Other Projects	31
New Management Company!	32
Two Management Companies	32
Should I Move?	33
Building Envelope Project	33
Big Tree is Gone	34
Extra Projects, Sidewalks and Lights	34
Lindy and the Ooogly Eyes	35
Letters from the Board	36
The Tractor is Stolen	36
The Hallway Fan Issue	37
Revised Policy Manual	38
Andy Being Evicted Again	39

Eviction of Another Neighbor 39
A New Member Upstairs 39
A New New Member Upstairs 40
The Start of my Demise - Noise from Electrical Room. 41
Advised to Call the Emergency Line 43
Next Electrician 43
Strange Man in my Unit 44
Severe Insomnia, High Blood Pressure and a Hernia 45
Call to the Bylaw Officers 46
Election Chaos 46
Definitely an Electrical Problem! 46
New President Harasses Me? 47
Agency Mocks Me 47
Electrical Conduit From Transformer To Building Damaged?. 48
Trying to Talk to Board Members 48
Sleeping in a Tent on My Patio 48
False Information to The Board 49
Acoustic Engineer Number Two 50
Elevator Noise Resolution 50
Acoustic Engineer Second Visit 50
Acoustic Report Confirms Noise 51
Management Company Report Error 52
Another Consultant 54
Filing a Case with The Civil Resolution Tribunal 54

7

CRT Meeting 55
After the CRT Meeting 56
Friendly Inspection of Units. 57
COVID Hits 57
So Much for Discussion 61
Victim Services Referral 62
Attempt to File the CRT Order in Courts 63
A Plea for Help 63
Covid Restrictions Lifted – Request to Honor CRT Order 68
Balcony Conversation Overheard by Theresa 69
Elevator Noise is Back 69
Another New Neighbor Across the Hall 69
CRT Complaints #2 and #3 70
Trying to Enforce CRT Order Leads to Termination 72
Response and presentation at the Board meeting regarding my Termination Meeting 72
    Preamble 73

    Addressing Claims: 74

    Enforcement of CRO Creates Bias of Board member and serious legal problem for co-op. 76

    Regarding Contact with Board and Obtaining Names and Addresses 76

    Noise Issues: 76

    Definition of Conduct Detrimental to the Co-op 77

    Particulars of the of the conduct complained of are: 78

Things I do as a member: 97
What does Termination accomplish? 98
In summary, ... 99
Terminated! I Appeal 101
Termination Meeting Announced! 101
An Offer to Resolve 102
CRT Complaints Stalled 106
I Find a New Place – It's Time To Leave 106
The Termination Meeting 107
Should I Appeal to the Supreme Court? 109
The Move-Out Inspection 109
Getting Ready for the Move-out Inspection 110
Elevator Noise Disappears 111
Threats from the Management Company 111
Encounter at the Grocery Store 112
Depression, Nightmares, High Blood Pressure 115
Collecting Monies Owed 115
A Government Roundtable Discussion on Reform 116
    Executive Summary 116
    My Summary and Experience 117
    Co-ops Are Forgotten 119
    Unlicensed Property Management Companies Operating Due to Loophole 119
    Eviction Protection During Covid 120

Access to Legal Representation 120
No Remedy for Members When Board Doesn't Follow Law. 120
Legislation Changes That Harmed Co-Ops 121
Quorum reduced from 20% to 15%. 122
Reduction of number of meetings: 122
Transparency Issues 123
Terminations and Timing of Meetings 123
The "Conduct Detrimental to the Co-op" Rule Harms Co-ops and Members 124
Some Co-ops Have Failed 125
Remedies Requested: 125

Outcome of the Meetings 126
A Revealing Search of Court Records 126
Another Encounter at the Grocery Store 126
Demand Letter Sent to Co-op 128
The Abusive FOI Response 130
Nightmares Continue 131
Resolution? 132
ChatGPT Analysis 132
Where Do I Go from Here? 137

Join a Housing Co-op. What Could Go Wrong?

The Offer

I had moved to Vancouver in 1995 to try to get accepted into the M. Ed in Counselling Psychology at UBC. The first few weeks I was living out of the Jericho Hostel with my belongings in my car, hoping that they would not be stolen as I looked for a place to live. I found a room with two women who were counsellors. That didn't work out well, as they had never had a male roommate and since both worked counselling abused women, the transference at play when they came home from work was quite high. A simple question such as "Is this your margarine or mine?" led to snappy reply. I lasted a month. In the meantime, I started socializing and made a new friend or two, one of which was a guy named Steve.

I found a new place which was a suite in the basement of the house. That lasted three months. I had found work as an instructor at a private school but was overwhelmed with the marking. I had also started a pre-requisite course at UBC and was busy with that. I received notice that I had been accepted into the Masters of Education in Counselling Psychology. I was also invited to give two presentations at a conference for counsellors in a few weeks. I finished the presentations and then went home to find that Michael, who held the lease for the house had not renewed it with the landlord. Tensions had been high in the house with conflict with his girlfriend, and arguments over the setting the thermostat and the resulting high heating bill. I found I had two weeks to find another place.

I had mentioned to my friend Steve that I needed to find a place. A few days later I received a call from Steve. He said that his former landlady had a place for rent and that I should call her immediately. He had called her to see if there was any mail for him and asked if she had any rooms or apartments for rent. She said she was just about to put an ad in the newspaper. I called immediately and she invited me to come right away. I went to meet her. The apartment was on the top floor of an older three-story home on the west side with a spectacular view of the mountains, Stanely Park, and the downtown skyline. The rent was only $500 but there was no stove, but I'd be allowed to use a hotplate. There was a full sized refrigerator, full bathroom, a separate bedroom, a dining area, large living room, and a small alcove with a the view of the north shore mountains and downtown.

Over the next seven years Toni and I became friends. She was in her 80's and my help to maintain the building, cutting grass, shoveling snow and fixing the occasional leaking pipe helped her stay in her home until her passing in 2002. I still keep in touch with her niece.

From there I moved to a stuffy basement suite in Kitsilano with no sunlight. My rent was now $850. I had heard about housing co-operatives over the years and had put in applications in various co-ops. In 2007 I got a call from a co-op that had a place for me. It was a massive 850 square foot one bedroom with a patio and nearby to SkyTrain and parks. I accepted the offer and moved in July 1st, 2007. My rent or housing charge as they called it was only $675 and the best thing was that they allowed pets which would allow me to keep my cat.

The moving in was strange. I was not contacted by the Co-op to arrange to get keys, and the membership committee members who had interviewed me seemed stressed when I called and quite formal and I could sense some sort of anxiety on their part. I managed to meet someone at the co-op office to get the keys, but come move-in day there was no one there to do the joint inspection of the unit.

I settled into the apartment and began meeting my neighbors. The second day I was asked if my unit was ok after the fire that morning. "What fire?" I asked. Apparently, the maintenance

Join a Housing Co-op. What Could Go Wrong?

person had arranged for some electrical work to be done, and it caused a fire. Fortunately, it had been contained in the electrical room below my unit. The maintenance person, David, had claimed that he shut off the power saving the building from further damage.

Now at the time, I had started to date my future wife. She helped me move into the co-op which being close to SkyTrain was convenient for her to visit me after work. I would get home about 30 minutes after she arrived at the complex, and she would wait patiently outside for me to come home. I felt it was uncomfortable for her to be waiting outside for me, so I got a set of keys made for the apartment and put them in a little jewelry box and left it on the second pillow on my bed for her to find. I was working away on my lesson plans, and she came and gave me a big hug. She had found the keys.

A few days later I was taking a nap and heard the door open and in came Anne with some suitcases. She thought that by giving her the keys, I had invited her to move in. Now, I had been single for quite a while and the prospect of someone moving in made me anxious, but I decided to go with the flow. She moved in and we were eager to enjoy our new co-op community and the beginnings of a great relationship together.

Minimal Elevator Noise

With our unit being directly above the elevator mechanical room, the boiler room and the electrical room, the only noise we could hear was a slight hum of the elevator when in operation. It was hardly noticeable.

Joining the Maintenance Committee

One of the principles of living in a co-op is member participation. I had been asked in my interview what committees I would like to join and I mentioned that I was handy with small repairs and would like to join the maintenance committee.

For weeks I heard nothing about joining the maintenance committed and inquired again a couple of times.

One evening I heard a knock at the door and answered. A man introduced himself as David and said he and his wife Libby were in charge of maintenance. We chatted for a while, and he said that he needed someone to be another maintenance person for the Co-op. We exchanged phone numbers.

A few days later he took me on a tour of the building.... The tool room, the boiler room, electrical room and explained other features of the building such as the security cameras. David and Libby said they wanted me to be an additional set of eyes and ears of the co-op. David handed me a set of master keys for the building. He also told me that the tool room could be my office and to make it comfortable, to make use of the desk, and put a stereo and personal items. He showed me the other tool room in another area in which he had a nice chair, stereo, and record collection. I could see that he had a number of ash trays and had been using it as a smoking room. In both tool rooms there were collections of light bulbs, light ballasts, and tools for the use of maintenance people like myself.

And so started my journey into hell.

David and William – History of Maintenance

The first thing I noticed about David was his lack of maintenance knowledge. Some of the older taps were dripping in some units, and instead of replacing a twenty-five-cent washer and sanding down any imperfections, he replaced the complete faucet. I mentioned that there was an easy way to fix them, but he said that he had already arranged for a bulk purchase of faucet sets.

The next thing I noticed was his ability to gossip about people. He told me the previous maintenance person, William, had been claiming to do repairs but pocketing the money instead. He also

Join a Housing Co-op. What Could Go Wrong?

told me that another previous maintenance person with master keys was seen by other members going into member's units when they weren't home. I didn't share this information.

David and Libby were very friendly at first and often asked me to check the camera recording for garbage left in the hallway or someone coming into the building. For the next year David and Libby and I were in almost daily contact to keep the co-op running smoothly.

Anne and I were now engaged. I had proposed to her at Christmas. We were hoping to switch to a two-bedroom unit and one came available. I toured the unit with David and saw that the previous tenants had left it in quite a mess. There were food stains on the wall. By now Libby had taken over the membership committee and was on the Board of Directors. Libby had explained to me that the previous membership committed, the couple I met at my initial meeting, had been removed because they had application files in their apartment and that was a privacy violation, so she took over the membership committee. The first thing Libby did was bring in her daughter who was assigned the two bedroom. The available two-bedroom was fully renovated with new flooring, kitchen cabinets and was freshly painted.

I also learned that David had been hired at one thousand dollars per month to look after maintenance. The two bedroom apartment was given to David and Libby's daughter who had two children.

As our wedding neared, we invited David and Libby to our wedding and reception, but on the day of our wedding they could not find the wedding pavilion and didn't show. Because I was teaching the summer semester, we planned our honeymoon for the fall.

Mark Linden O'Meara

Conflict Starts

A few months after the wedding things started to sour between David, Libby and me. One day the front automatic door stopped working. David called me to check the camera footage which I did and saw that his contractor had put a garbage pail to block the door from closing so he could come in and out easily. David insisted I was wrong. I told him the cameras don't lie. A day later the door was opening very slowly. Later in the day there was a loud bang, and the door was knocked off its railing. Again, David called asking me to check the cameras and find out who had damaged the door. David said very explicitly that he would "nail the mother fucker who did it". I checked the cameras and found that it was his legally blind son-in-law who had banged into the door, but only because the door was not opening properly and he couldn't see that. David swore up and down that I was wrong. Again, I told him to check himself. He did, and of course, since it was a relative, he took no action. Another time I was asked to find out who had left some cabinets in the basement area and telling him who it was, he said "Oh, never mind.... Those are nice people" Another incident to be checked was to find out who had left garbage near the elevator. I checked the cameras and found it was his daughter and granddaughter, to which he replied, "No it must be someone else."

As the maintenance committee member, it was my responsibility to notice things that needed to be repaired and to submit work orders. I had noticed that the door at the end of the garage was not closing properly. The locking mechanism was damaged and was keeping the door open. I submitted multiple work orders over the next while because of the susceptibility to someone getting into the garage and breaking into cars. Well, the lock was never repaired and one morning we found that eleven cars had been broken into. My expensive sound system had been ripped out of my car. I explained to other members that I had

Join a Housing Co-op. What Could Go Wrong?

submitted a work order to get that lock fixed, but nothing happened. David and Libby released a letter to all members stating that the break in had been an "inside job" but no rationale was given for this conclusion.

Another problem I had been experiencing with David was that he was not good at respecting boundaries. He seemed to be very lonely and was knocking on my door almost every night, sometimes twice, to walk around the building to do a ground inspection. He wanted to start nightly security rounds. My wife Anne was getting annoyed that he was knocking at the door every night disturbing our time together. A few times that he knocked I said I was busy and could not go out to do these inspections. I spoke to David saying that we should set up times to work on maintenance, perhaps one night or two nights a week, but that at other times he should not knock on my door. Despite my boundary setting, he continued to repeatedly knock on my door a couple of times per week.

In one of our maintenance talks, David mentioned that he wanted to trim the bushes around the co-op. I mentioned that the bushes outside our unit gave us privacy, being a ground floor apartment near the entrance to the building. I asked him not to cut the bushes in front of our unit.

Anne and I went on our honeymoon to China. Upon our return, as the taxi from the airport pulled up to the co-op, we could see that the bushes in front of our unit had been all cut down to almost nothing. All that remained were sticks.

Now that everyone could see into our unit if the curtains were open, I wrote to the Board asking if we could plant a hedge to block the sightline, explaining that David had cut down all the bushes when we were away.

The next time I saw David there was a deep look of betrayal on his face and he would not talk to me. I had no idea that telling the board what he had done and requesting a remedy would trigger such a deep display of pain and emotion. I could see in his eyes that it was like I had pulled the rug out from under him. I heard from other members that he was now bad mouthing me and starting rumors about me.

The Reputation Attacking Begins

Over the next few weeks, I heard from other co-op members that he was telling them to watch out for me and that I was a snake I the grass. Other members started opening up to me about how he had treated others and about his lack of any formal training in maintenance.

I learned that William had been the former maintenance manager. He had significant maintenance experience and had kept maintenance costs at a minimum. I heard that in the year prior to my moving into the co-op, David and Libby had gotten divorced Now divorced and broke, Libby had no money for food. Some co-op members such as William stepped in to help and bring her food.

At this time apparently, there was talk about evicting David and Libby, but all the parties reconciled after a healing meeting in the park. All was forgiven, but David and Libby needed a source of income. They proceeded to commandeer the maintenance of the co-op. William was trying to get repairs done, but he was told by his contractors that they had been instructed to only speak to David and Libby. With no contractors, he could not do the maintenance work and quit as the maintenance coordinator. Now a clearer picture of the politics of the co-op was emerging.

Reconciliation?

A few weeks later David and I had a talk. He said that he felt I was a friend and didn't want conflict. I expressed my concern that he was sharing negative talk about me. We seemed to patch things up and shook hands, but a few days later I heard that he was still talking negatively about me. The "little kids shaking hands and apologizing" didn't seem to last.

Scrutiny of Finances and Maintenance.

A co-op is supposed to be founded on the principles of transparency, accountability, and member involvement. Many of us were finding ourselves frustrated that we could not find out any information about what we were spending money on. Maintenance work was being done by friends of David and Libby, and some of the work was thought to be completely unnecessary. We also weren't happy that some people were getting preferential treatment.

A group of five of us, plus myself, formed an ad hoc committee that wanted to steer the co-op into a better management position. We requested all the maintenance invoices for the last year and were surprised that we were actually given access to them. We discovered that three friends of David and Libby had been given work in excess of twenty thousand dollars each. Some of the invoices were questionable, such as sixteen hundred dollars to replace a toilet. The toilet only cost one hundred and fifty dollars so we were wondering why the invoice was so high.

As a group we released a report to the members requesting that the Board set up a finance committee, and a maintenance committee. We met with the Board to discuss our findings but none of our concerns were acted upon.

One of the major concerns was that there was no segregation of duties. David and Libby decided what work was to be done, chose the contractor, and approved payment. The only other stage was that the check was signed by the treasurer. With my knowledge of accounting principles and my teaching Accounting Information Systems, this lack of segregation of duties would easily allow for fraud to occur in any organization. Segregation of duties is a basic practice in accounting practices and financial management of an organization to prevent fraud. These issues were raised at a meeting, but the Board dismissed these concerns. One Board member said there were no segregation of duties at her workplace which was a large entity in the region.

Another major concern was that the Co-op had hired David to manage maintenance, but the Co-op was paying Libby, allegedly so David could avoid reporting income to social services and a Workmen's Compensation claim. Libby was being paid as a contractor even though she was an employee of the co-op, leaving the co-op liable for back taxes and payroll deductions.

In the meantime. Libby had been removed from the Board by the auditor based on the rules that a Board member is ineligible if another member in the unit is a paid employee or derives work from the Co-op. Next thing we know, we are changing auditors.

Sensing a lack of accountability, and on the advice of a co-op organization it was suggested that we attempt a coup by running a slate of candidates at the next election. Libby told me that they were aware there was a Group A and Group B and that anyone trying to change the governance wouldn't succeed because they had a lot of friends in the co-op, I started to learn what "friends" meant. One member who was on the Board flooded her apartment because she put cat litter down the toilet. The unit needed flooding remediation and a new carpet. David and Libby, being the kind people they are, arranged for her not to have to pay the bill. Another lady on the second floor accidentally started a grease fire in her kitchen but again the bill for repairs was "taken care of."

We were acutely aware of some sketchy behaviors by the co-op. Another break in the garage occurred and a senior's garage remote was either lost or stolen. David and Libby called in the

Join a Housing Co-op. What Could Go Wrong?

garage door company to reset the codes, but they waited until after hours so that the invoice would be billed at overtime rates. She was threatened with termination if she didn't pay the bill which was a couple of hundred dollars.

The Co-op Tractor

The co-op had bought a John Deer tractor to plow the snow and a trailer for distributing road salt. Our policy manual stated that any unbudgeted purchase over two thousand dollars needed to be brought to the membership, but that never happened.

David now realized they needed to build an enclosure for the tractor. A parking space was selected next to a tool room to be converted to a shed to house the tractor. Both Anne and I assisted David in the building of the shed, but when some nails, wood, and paint was ordered, the wrong items were delivered to the co-op. I was sitting in David and Libby's kitchen when Libby called the lumber supply company to complain. I was shocked at how she yelled and tore a strip of the person in customer service who took the call. I thought to myself that I should distance myself from the co-op when dealing with the lumber supply store or any other vendors. Libby expressed a lot of anger for the mix up. I was not able to confirm, but another member reported a few days later that he was at the lumber supply store and saw that David had started to aggressively chew out a store employee. Allegedly the police were called and David was escorted out of the store and told not to return.

An Elevator from Hell

On a Friday afternoon I heard a horrible grinding noise coming from below our apartment. Upon investigation, I found that when the elevator went up to the third floor, the equipment in the elevator room below our unit made a horrible grinding noise. A sound like a bear growling and metal crunching as gears grinded without oil or lubricant.

I called David and Libby to report the issue saying that if the elevator goes to the third floor, the equipment under our unit makes a horrible grinding noise. About thirty minutes later I get a call from Libby stating that everything is fine. I tell her it's clearly not and explain again that we can hear the noise clearly in our apartment every time the elevator goes to the third floor. Libby starts yelling at me saying I said the noise was on the third floor. I told her that is not what I said. She starts yelling at me "You have communication problems! If you had only explained it carefully! Blah blah blah. I hang up on her. About an hour later David knocks on my door and says "Yes there's an elevator problem. The gears are low on fluid. I'll call them on Monday." I tell him that with that kind of sound we won't be able to sleep and that significant damage will occur to the elevator. He replies that he's not going to call them until Monday. We can't sleep all weekend. I am unable to find a Board member till Monday morning, but when I do I knock on his door and ask him to come to my unit to hear the noise. He comes down a little later and while he is in my unit I go to the elevator and press the third-floor button, jump out of the elevator and rush back to my unit. Eugene hears the loud noise and is startled by it. I tell him that this is what we have had to put up with for the whole weekend because David and Libby would not call the elevator company. He assures me he'll get right on it. The elevator is fixed the next day.

Master Keys and Store Accounts

Now at this time, I still have the master keys to the whole building. I asked David if I could store a Xmas present for Anne in the tool room, and that it would be out of the way. He replied that it was ok, as I had full use of the facilities and that the tool room was mine to make my own. I had also asked if I could put

Join a Housing Co-op. What Could Go Wrong?

my exercise bike in the tool room and he said it was ok. There were a few times I came into the tool room to use it, but it was in use by his daughter. She also had keys to the tool room and had left some tires, and some garbage bags of old toys in the tool room. I mentioned to David that the tool room was getting quite messy with all of his daughter's storage items.

I had stored a present for Anne in the electrical room with David's permission - a bean bag chair that was too big to hide in our apartment. But I was now hobbling around with my injured knee. Libby called and said that they have a contractor coming in the next day and that I have to remove everything from the tool room. I manage to do so, but with a great deal of pain.

I sensed that this was a retaliatory action by David and Libby for complaining about all the garbage their daughter was leaving in the tool room. I also remembered how David and Libby had accused a former maintenance person of going into people's units with the master keys. Intuition told me that I should immediately return the master keys. I went to visit the co-op president, resigned from the maintenance committee and handed in the keys to her. Sensing that I might be accused of various issues as others had, I had my name removed from the co-op contractor accounts at the local building supply stores. I made sure that my name was not tied to the co-op credit card issued to David and Libby. Only a few select members were aware that the co-op had a credit card issued to David and Libby.

Wasting Road Salt

On the next snowfall, the tractor got stuck trying to move the smallest amount of snow with the snow plow attachment. It could not move even the smallest amount of snow so the snow attachment was removed and was to be used for distributing road salt on the driveway and walkways. David loaded the full pallet of road salt into the trailer attachment and drove around the building to drop some salt on the driveway and walkways. He had unloaded the full pallet of road salt, a 5 x 5 x 5 pallet into the trailer. Unfortunately, he had incorrectly adjusted the flow and by the time he completed his salting run, he had released the full load onto the sidewalk. We now had no road salt for the rest of the year.

The light above our locker in the locker room stopped working. I put in a work order, but nothing happened. It was frustrating trying to get things out of our locker in pitch darkness. After a month I put in another work order, again nothing happened. We rarely had meetings, but at the next meeting I asked about getting the light fixed. The president made some excuse and that I should just use a flashlight. Another member spoke up and said, "It should be fixed" But it never got fixed until a year later when they replaced all the light fixtures in the basement and parking garage. Again, we were concerned that money was being spent without consultation of the membership. The annual maintenance budget did not contain any line items of what was planned for the year so projects like this went ahead without any scrutiny.

Fast Forward to Next Summer:

Fellow members Roger and his wife went on vacation and when they returned their toilet was blocked. Although the issue was discovered at 2pm, the drain company wasn't called in until after 5 pm the next day again resulting in overtime rates. Some wipes were discovered to be the cause of the blockage but there was also some flushable cat litter in the pipes. Roger was given a bill for a couple of thousand dollars. He disputed the bill, taking the co-op to small claims court, asking that his debt to the co-op be reduced due to the inflation of the bill for unnecessary overtime billing and disputing the length of the pipe that was replaced.

Join a Housing Co-op. What Could Go Wrong?

Because we had distributed our report about the financial concerns and our desire to form committees (our co-op had no committees) the camera in the lobby had been directed away from the entrance to the mailboxes to monitor anyone putting anything in the mailboxes. The Board issued a notice that only Board approved notices could be left in mailboxes or on bulletin boards.

Unfortunately, no one who ran on our platform for the elections got elected except one person. Roger was nominated but immediately disqualified by the board because he had an outstanding amount owing to the co-op because he was challenging the co-op's bill in small claims court, claiming it was over-inflated.. He protested saying it was a fabricated charge and that he was fighting it in court and should be allowed to run. The board would not let his nomination stand.

The one member of our team who got elected, Victor, was told he could not attend meetings because he had supported the document we had created and was part of our team now labelled as disruptive. He knew this because they forgot that they had included him in the board email list and an email was sent by the President to all board members that he was not to be invited to attend Board meetings. He did manage to find out the time and location of one meeting and attended but they refused to listen to him or allow him to vote.

Fixing a Camera Leads to Removal

A few days later Victor noticed that a camera at the entrance of the building was loose and pointing at the ground. He adjusted the camera to point to the door and tightened the adjusting screw. A few days later he got an invoice from David's son-in-law's company to repair the camera. The invoice was for a couple of hundred dollars. Disputing the bill, he demanded a copy of the invoice, which stated that the old camera could be reused. Based on this the bill was reduced by the co-op to fifty dollars but Victor refused to pay it saying he had not done any harm to co-op property and that there was nothing wrong with the camera. At the next AGM he was removed from the Board because of this outstanding invoice and his position was put up for election, or rather acclamation. Nobody ran for any of the board positions.

We were clearly disappointed with the results of our efforts to improve management at the co-op, and as a final effort we decided to print copies of The CMHC Guide to Good Governance and distribute them to members. We distributed them one afternoon, leaving them at the doors of members. A few hours later almost all the copies were dropped back at my door with the words "Fuck You" written on the top of the pile. A few hours later I was visited by the RCMP who said they had a complaint from a member that I was harassing the members by leaving documents at their door or in their mailbox. I explained to the officer that it was a group of us who did this and that I was not the only person involved in this effort.I also explained that it was a guide for co-op management published by the government. I was asked to provide my identification. The officer told me not to distribute these guides or anything else. I reminded him that it was a group effort. The officer made no attempt to ascertain the names of the other group members.

Noisy Garage Fan Conflict

The garage of the co-op had a series of three large fans on timers that would turn on for an hour or so based on timer settings. The timers were in the electrical room. One day I was in the electrical room with David, and he changed the settings of the fan timers. They were manually adjusted times with little pins that determined the time the fans came on and off. A dial would spin to set the correct time.

Join a Housing Co-op. What Could Go Wrong?

The fans had not been maintained – belts needed to be adjusted or replaced every so often and this hadn't been done recently. I observed a fan assembly shaking crazily and reported it to David and Libby, but Libby again just yelled at me.

A few days later all there was some maintenance done on the fans. New belts were installed, but David had turned on the fans 24/7. These were massive fans and very noisy. Some people could no longer talk on their balconies and had to close their windows to block out the noise. Complaints were filed at the Co-op office, but nothing was done about this. Of course, the fan near a board member's unit was left off. All the other fans were left blaring.

The cost of the electricity being consumed by these fans was presented by some members at a fall meeting, and I spoke up and said that all they had to do to solve this was to put the fans back on the timers. Libby was at the meeting and said, "There are no timers!" I was written up in the minutes as "One member claimed there were fan timers".

At a subsequent meeting where the noise of the fans was raised again, I again stated that I had been in the electrical room as a maintenance person and had observed the timers. This time the President snapped at me and said "Mark, again, there are no timers. Let's settle this once and for all. David, are there timers?" David answered "Yes, there are timers" to the shock of the president. Her jaw dropped. I wasn't making this up after all. But then David added, "but we were having to replace the belts every week." I had been on the maintenance committee and knew this was a lie. The number of belts required to replace the 6 fans in total times 52 weeks would be an exorbitant expense and effort and would have been noticed. The fans stayed on despite the protests of members.

Members are having to sleep with their windows closed in the heat of summer to reduce the noise from the fans. Meanwhile,

17

Victor went out onto his balcony his foot went through the floor. Obviously there needs to be some major repairs to the co-op.

The Whir, Whir, Whir Fan

Since the earlier elevator noise had been repaired, our apartment had been relatively quiet, even though we were about the elevator mechanical room, the electrical room and the boiler room. We started to hear a slight motor noise when the elevator when up to the third floor, but everything was relatively quiet until we started to hear a humming noise that varied slightly in pitch —I filled out a work order, but nothing was done. The work order was returned to me stating that all the equipment was working correctly.

For two weeks we were bothered by this noise and had trouble sleeping, especially Anne. David refused to fix it. I went to the President, and she agreed to come into our apartment. She could clearly hear the noise. Anne politely asked her to deal with David and try to get it fixed as we did not hear the noise when we first moved in. I suggested getting help from outside the co-op, to which she agreed.

A few days later an electrician was brought in, and he identified the problem within a few minutes. A boiler room ventilation fan's bearings were worn out and causing the vibration. The fan was attached to a cement wall right underneath our living room. As soon as the fan was turned off the noise stopped. A replacement fan with better sound insulation mounts was installed.

Afterwards, the President came to visit unexpectedly. She strongly suggested that we find another place to live as she believed we weren't co-op candidates. We described all the work we did on a weekly basis and that we were valuable members of the co-op and were on good terms with many members.

A few weeks later there was a general meeting and I asked to speak. I wanted to address the issue of maintenance at the co-op

Join a Housing Co-op. What Could Go Wrong?

and what I had to do to get work orders dealt with, specifically the boiler room fan issue. I was given a chance to speak, but as soon as I opened my mouth, all of the Board members simultaneously started yelling gibberish so no one could hear what I was saying. When I sat down, they stopped. I left the meeting in disgust.

News Breaks

News breaks that the large organization that our board member works at was the victim of a massive fraud that was going on for years because there was poor segregation of duties. Fake companies were created along with fake invoices, and millions of dollars had been siphoned over the years. So much for the President's defense of our own co-op's lack of segregation of duties because "we don't even do that at our workplace!"

The lack of segregation of duties had been reported to the auditor but now we are changing auditors again. David and Libby are searching for a new auditor.

Flooded Unit

It is reported that a member came home to find their sinks plugged and taps turned on full flooding their apartment. There is no sign of forced entry.

Bang Bang—It's not the Compressor.

It just started one day.... In the middle of the night, around three a.m. The sound was something similar to a sledgehammer hitting a metal beam.... bang, bang, bang, bang, bang.... It went on for about three minutes then abruptly stopped. Anne wasn't woken up by it. From her shift work as a nurse in China she could sleep through anything.

It happened again two days later. I reported the issue on a work order, but the work order was returned to me with the standard "Everything working fine." I could hear it was coming from the boiler room which also had the dry fire sprinkler system and a compressor to maintain air pressure for the system.

I spoke to the local Fire Department who advised me that there was likely an air leak in the dry sprinkler system and that our maintenance people should investigate that as the cause of the compressor coming on. I submitted another work order but again it came back with the same response. I wrote to the Board. By now David and Libby were not speaking to me but had asked another Board member, Polly to liaise with me. She knocked on my door and told me that David said that there was nothing in the equipment rooms that could make that kind of noise. She said, "David says it's not the compressor."

A few days later the fire alarm goes off. I'm out in the hallway and after it's determined that it is a false alarm. I speak to one of the firemen and ask, "Can you inspect our sprinkler system because the compressor keeps going off and your office said there is likely a slow air leak." Polly is standing nearby, and she yells at me "Mark O'Meara, I am a Board Member, and I order you to go back to your unit right now!" The fireman looks at us both. I look at Polly and state "Polly, you are a Board member. You have the right to vote, but you do not have the authority to order people like this." Her jaw drops. The fireman states that we should call in the company that manages our fire equipment.

A few days later I see David coming towards me as I'm walking into the building. He's walking with one of his contractors. This is a contractor who reported a conversation back to David and Libby when I asked why we were painting all the doors in the basement and garage resulting in a letter from the board telling me not to harass contractors. I speak to David calmly and ask him to investigate the compressor more fully and resolve this issue because it is waking us up. He starts yelling at me angrily, telling me to stop bothering him. Three days later I got a letter from the

Join a Housing Co-op. What Could Go Wrong?

co-op lawyer stating that I have violated the rules of the co-op and the good neighbor rules for abusive behavior towards David. I am advised to change my behavior or face termination.

The noise continues for some weeks. It's now October and any work orders I submit are ignored. I approach the co-op president asking for either outside help since this has worked in the past or preferably mediation. Fortunately, the Board agrees to mediation. Even though this is waking us up, it's going to take a few weeks to arrange mediation. Our first mediation meeting happens in November.

In mediation, the co-op president agrees to work to determine and confirm the cause of the noise. David will not be involved. A few days later, I am in my apartment and a person from the fire sprinkler company turns on the compressor. That's the noise. The Fire Protection company does it's annual maintenance work and finally the noise stops. We now have a mediation agreement in place that the work order process will be respected by all parties and that any issue that can cause harm to a member's health will be deemed an emergency.

In the final meeting, the co-op president raises some new concerns that I was taking liberties with the tool room. I explained to her that I was only following what David and Libby had told me and that conflict started when I complained about David and Libby's daughter making a mess in the tool room with her stuff. I told the President that Lindy has a key to the tool room and the President counters saying that she needs the key to access the vacuum cleaner to do her weekly job unit. I explain to the President that people are complaining that she doesn't do her weekly job unit of vacuuming but instead uses the co-op vacuum cleaner to clean her car. The president apologizes. Anne also raises the issue that Polly continually misquotes her as saying that the noise doesn't bother her. Anne clarifies that the noise is a problem but that she said that because she was a night shift nurse she can easily fall back asleep but that it bothers both of us. The President apologies for this too.

Fix a Leak -Accused of Making a Mess

Anne and I had been involved in gardening in the co-op, cutting the grass and had a key to the garden tool room next to the lobby. A water supply was needed for watering the plants in the courtyard so David installed a hose in the garden tool room. This room has no floor drain. I notice the hose dripping and soaking into the wall. At that moment I noticed the only thing stopping water is the nozzle at the end of the hose. I lift up to the nozzle and the whole thing pops off and water is spraying everywhere. I shut off the water and noticed that David had installed the wrong type of hose fitting on the end of the hose and it wasn't properly clamped and tightened. I head off to the hardware store and get the proper parts and fix the hose. I had to rush off to my class, so I close up the garden tool room and head to school. When I return home all the hose parts are at my front door with all the gardening tools dumped at my door. I put them all back at the door of the garden tool room. I go to talk to the President, and she says that someone made a 'mess' and David had to clean it up. She defends him saying "How do you know it was him?" I reply, "He's the only other person with the key to that room." She goes silent.

Front Lawn Destruction

During the winter our co-op lawn is destroyed by contractors driving on our lawn. The building grounds look terrible. I spoke to one driver who said David told him to park his truck on the lawn.

Despite complaints by members regarding contractors driving their vehicles on the lawn, it continues. The front of the building looks terrible.

Join a Housing Co-op. What Could Go Wrong?

David Riles Up My Neigbour

Summer comes and goes.... A few minor incidents but one major one comes to mind. My neighbor had driven his van up onto the lawn right outside our patio and bedroom window. I see him talking to David and David keeps nodding towards our unit. David leaves but it's now 11:30pm and he's still unloading metal from his van. I went to talk to him to ask politely if he could try to do this at an earlier time because Anne is sleeping and has to be up early. He starts to get out of his vehicle and comes towards me in anger ready to punch me. It seems David really stirred him up against me. He starts yelling at me. Why do you let your friends come through your patio to visit you? Why can't they come through the front door? You wake my kids up. I told him I didn't know we were bothering him and would ask my stepdaughter and any other friends not to do this. I move away and he continues to unload. It's not safe to be near him.

Anne and I advise all our friends and our stepdaughter to come in through the front door and to exit from the building front door. But my neighbor no longer makes eye contact with us and gives us the silent treatment.

A few months later I go to get into my car and noticed that he's sitting in his van with the engine running. By now the garage fans have been turned off pending the installation of some new fans and automatic controls. He's been in his older van and has been running it for quite a while. I'm concerned that he might succumb to carbon monoxide, so I go to his van window. I told him the garage fans are not working and there is no air circulation so to be careful of the exhaust. From then on, he is nicer to me, saying hello in the hallway.

Anne and have received approval to install laminate flooring in our unit. I am cutting the boards on a table saw on our patio. We usually stop by ten pm. After a few days' work, the same neighbor comes to us around 9:30pm asking us if we could stop earlier because his kids go to bed at eight pm. I say "Oh, I have one more board to cut for tonight, then change my mind and stop for the night. For the remainder of the work, we stop at eight pm even though it delays the completion of our flooring. A few months later he moves out having been able to save enough to buy a house.

Bang, Bang, Bang Part III

Things have been relatively quiet… but now it's fall and then bang, bang, bang….The compressor noise has started up again.

I submitted another work order but again nothing happens. I emailed Libby and she says she will contact the Fire Management Company. I get an email back suggesting they move the compressor from near the ceiling to mid-way up the wall, but for some reason the email contains the statement from the Fire Management Company that "this is by no means urgent!" I remind the co-op of the Mediation Agreement, that this is harming my health, and they are in breach of the mediation agreement.

We have a new co-op president, Gillian, and I go to see her before a meeting. I calmly ask her to investigate and fix the issue, and she escalates the issue raising her voice and stating, "There is no noise!" I remain calm and advise her that if the co-op won't fix the issue, I will have to sue the co-op. She escalates her voice further and yells, "Go ahead, see you in court!"

I file a lawsuit against the co-op and the Fire System management company to force them to fix the issue. The co-op hires a lawyer who calls me and says he will help mediate. At first, he is friendly and seems to want to resolve things but then starts to berate me for "trying to change the way the co-op is managed." He also tells me that I can't win the case. I ask why, and he says that I have asked for things in my court filing that Small Claims

Join a Housing Co-op. What Could Go Wrong?

Court cannot order. I go to Small Claims Court and remove that clause from the case filing. I get a call from him the next day that he has received the updated case and we see each other and court. I tell him my case is now winnable. He says he noticed that with quite a strong sense of embarrassment. I may have taught him a very valuable lesson to not reveal his legal strategy to the opposing party! I re-iterate that if the co-op were to resolve the issue, I would drop the lawsuit. The lawyer seems uninterested in resolving the issue and again berates me for trying to change the management of the co-op.

Garage Door Comes Down on a Guy's Vehicle

A garage door malfunctioned and came down on a member's van. David and Gillian claim that he should have gotten out of the van and swung his foot out to retrigger the garage door laser trigger to keep the door open. The co-op sues him, and he goes to court. He tells me a few weeks later that he won the case. Gillian claimed that she was a witness, but the judge almost sanctioned her for lying because although she claimed to be a witness, she wasn't in any of the videos that captured the accident. David also was criticized by the judge because he claimed that as part of the orientation for new members, he would teach them how to reset the door laser by putting their foot out in front of the laser beam that triggered the door opening or resetting. Although he won his case, in the end Gillian and David filed an insurance claim on the guy's automobile policy even though the court denies he's liable. He tells me he just doesn't want to fight it anymore. A few days later his laptops were stolen from his apartment without any sign of forced entry.

Bang, Bang, Bang continued.

David tells me that he brought in the Fire Protection System Company and that they found nothing wrong with the compressor and that they performed a detailed inspection.

I have included the Fire Protection System Company in the lawsuit to get their attention. I call to speak to a manager at the company but he tells me that they have not been told of any problem and that the previous service call David mentioned was not an inspection but a training session for David to explain to him how the system worked. I pleaded with him to come in to fix the issue because the noise was keeping me up at night and I was now suffering from severe insomnia. I had provided doctors notes to the co-op as well. He stated that he could not come in unless the co-op asked them to come in. David was refusing to call them in, instead, waiting for the annually scheduled inspection in January. It was currently November. For the next two months I was awoken every two nights by the compressor. I kept a log of the timing and found it was going off every 32 hours.

Finally, the inspection occurred and the Fire System Protection company replaced a hose for $300 including labor that was the cause of a small air leak that was causing the compressor to come on when the pressure dropped below a trigger point.

Since it was now resolved, I dropped the lawsuit as I had promised.

Garage Leak Repairs – Are we Being Hosed?

The Co-op has hired a company to repair leaks in the garage. There are cracks in the foundation. Roger provides information that the company hired, who is a friend of David and Libby is not reputable as they failed to properly do the work on another client's garage repairs. They are going to jackhammer the cracks open and fill them with cement. The cost of the project is exorbitant and members raise concerns that we are being overcharged. Despite our concerns, the work begins. We find out they are just general laborers being paid minimum wage. The project was providing a significant profit for the repair company. Some of us complain that this should not be patched from inside the garage but that it should be properly patched from outside the foundation. The repairs stop the water for a couple of months but then all the leaks return. The work will have to be redone during a building envelope repair.

The AGM – No Elections

We have an AGM but I'm away travelling. At the AGM we adopted a new set of co-op rules to comply with updated legislation. I learn on my return that no elections have occurred. Half of the Board should have their positions reaffirmed or new members should be elected. The Board has decided that because we had adopte new rules, the term limits have been reset. It was pointed out that the new rules explicitly state that this is not the case. The new Board just stays on without elections. Many neighbors express that it doesn't really matter because almost every Board elected in the last ten years has been elected by acclamation! No one seems to notice that the Grievance Policy section of the new rules simply states "Not Applicable."

Roger Moves - Can't Close Financing.

Roger loses his court case. His small claims case was heard at the end of the day by a substitute judge filling in because the regular judge is sick. Despite following all the rules, he was not allowed to call witness and was cut short when trying to explain that he was not denying liability but was challenging the amount of the bill. He tells me once he said he was not denying liability, the judge said he didn't want to hear any more and ordered full payment without hearing from witnesses or his claim to reduce the bill. He is ordered to pay the bill. He pays the bill quickly.

Roger tells me he and his wife have bought a home will move shortly. At the last minute his financing has fallen apart and cannot secure his financing under his name. Even though he paid his outstanding co-op invoice on time, the co-op has reported him to the credit bureau for not paying on time. His credit rating has been badly damaged, and he has to scramble to put the financing in his wife's name. Roger moves out. We share a coffee in his apartment to say goodbyes.

More Bullying to a Different Member

It's now summer. A few incidents occur. The garage fans have been turned off and replaced with new equipment. A neighbor gets new flooring installed and some repairs done by Davd and Libby's contractor friend, but now his closet door is scraping on the floor and going. He puts in a work order and the same contractor shows up and starts arguing with him. My neighbor says he was calm. The door doesn't get fixed and the contractor leaves. My neighbor gets a letter from the Board accusing him of being hostile to the contractor.

Elevator Noise Starts to Get Bothersome

Ever since the elevator grinding noise was repaired, the noise we can hear in our unit has gotten louder and louder. I put in a work order describing the sound and how we didn't hear it when we moved in.

I get the work order back in my mailbox. David and Libby reply that the elevator is working normally. Nothing is to be done. I'm not up for another fight at the moment. We learn to get used to the elevator noise.

Meetings and Mediators

All meetings, as rare as they are, now occur with a mediator present. The mediator asks for committee reports. I put up my

Join a Housing Co-op. What Could Go Wrong?

hand and am recognized to speak. I tell the mediator that we can skip committee reports because we have no committees. She looks baffled and moves on. It seems everything has already been decided before the meeting occurs. Despite numerous topics discussed, there is nothing to vote on.

After one meeting while taking the elevator, I'm told by a Board member to "go back to where I came from." The mediator is in the elevator and shuts down this talk. A few months later the Board member moved out. He was sued by the co-op for thousands of damages to the unit. In the court documents he states that he went through a move out inspection and no issues were raised. He also stated that the date of the inspection on the notice of service was one month after he moved out. The replies and counter claims back and forth, but on the court date neither the co-op representative nor the co-op lawyer show up. The case is dismissed.

Andy's Harassment and Attempted Eviction

My disabled low-income neighbor Andy gets a notice that his subsidy was calculated incorrectly and that he owes a balance of a couple of hundred dollars. He gets a notice that his membership will be terminated if he doesn't pay up. He works out a payment plan and pays it off, but the Co-op is still pursuing the termination. He asks for help, and I suggest he get a legal advocate. Gillian seems to really have it in for him and so does David and Libby. He was part of our team that analyzed the co-ops' financial transactions and tried to run for the Board. The advocate gets involved and shows the co-op that the termination is illegal and cannot proceed. The Board backs off.

Shrubs Cut Again

I'm working from home, and I see a contractor coming up to the bushes outside my unit. David had decided to cut them back again. No other work is being done. I ask him and the contractor to stop but David tells him not to stop. I call the Police asking them to intervene. They show up but say there is nothing they can do. I explain that he is trying to bug me by doing this. The contractor continues and now all I have above my patio fence are sticks protruding into the air. The nice green shrubs are gone. I come back out and ask the contractor to trip further down so I don't see the sticks. David tells him not to do it.

Neighbor Floods Her Apartment

One morning I heard a gurgling sound coming from my kitchen sink. I checked the bathroom as well and heard the same sound. I went out of my unit to the courtyard. Don was attending a nearby unit. Angela was outside of her unit. I could see from the open door that the unit had flooded from an overflowing bathtub and was continuing to flood. It was flooding with water and sewage. Obviously, the collector drain underneath the floor in the basement was blocked. Apparently, Angela had been putting used cat litter down her toilet, and it had blocked the pipe. I told David that he needed to shut off the water so that the water from showers and other use would not back up into other units. He told me to go back to my unit and refused to turn off the water. I went back into my apartment and sewage was now backing up in our bathtub. It was food particles and who knows what else. I had to leave to go teaching. I told David that our bathtub was filling up with sewage and again stressed that he needed to turn off the water.

Angela had flooded her unit due to putting cat litter down the toilet. All the carpeting and flooring had to be replaced. They did a very nice job over the next few weeks. She never got a bill for the damage – the bill was 'taken care of' and so began Angela's loyalty to David and Libby.

Join a Housing Co-op. What Could Go Wrong?

Saving The Tree

A few months later I hear a chainsaw going. David is having the low-lying branches cut on the beautiful tall tree that gives us some protection from the SkyTrain noise. He has already cut all the branches to about eight feet above ground. I go up to a Board members unit, Andreas, and explain what he's doing. He explains that the low-level branches need to be cut so they can trim the lawn. I agree with him that this is necessary, but I tell him that David has already gone as high as eight feet. The Board member, Andreas, comes out looks in horror at what he has David and tells him to stop.

A few weeks later the police are out front of the building. Apparently, Andreas got a parking ticket for being parked in a no parking zone near the front of the co-op. He decided to get a ladder and tools to remove the "No Parking" sign but someone reported him to the police. The police were supervising his work to put the sign back.

Building Envelop and Other Projects

We've been advised that the building envelope needs to be repaired as there are leaks and possible rot. The Co-op hires a company to remedy the specific areas needing repair. Patchwork repairs are done, but a few months later we are advised that the whole building envelope needs to be replaced. A contractor is hired to manage the project, but they report that supplies are being billed to the co-op that were delivered and then removed to another site. Some members had their windows removed, but the replacement windows were measured incorrectly and didn't fit. One member and his family were left with no windows during freezing weather during the Christmas holidays. The work finishes but we are now being advised that those repairs did not work, and we need a completely new building refit.

The Board presents a budget for the project. Our current Management Company will manage the project for us. It involves removing and replacing the building envelope, repairing any rot, replacing balconies, new windows and balcony doors, and a plumbing retrofit as the current copper piping is springing leaks. There will also be a new garage ventilation system.

New Management Company!

Apparently, we have a new management company. Without any consultation of the membership, the current president Gillian has signed an agreement with a different Management Company allegedly going against the Board's wishes to stay with the current company.

At our annual AGM, the budget shows that the new company will be charging us at least three times what the old company charged us. There will be additional costs for maintenance.

The first mistake the new management company makes is failing to withdraw charges for extra parking spaces. Instead of getting a letter advising us about the issue and how to get it resolved, we get notices that we are in arrears and our membership could be terminated if we don't pay up immediately.

The Renovation project proceeds.... Two years of disruption... walls and ceilings are cut open to install new plumbing,

Two Management Companies

The previous management company was contracted to oversea the building envelope project under a separate contract. Now we have a new company to manage the co-op and somehow there is confusion. A legal dispute arises because the old management company claims it is responsible for the management of the building envelope project and allowing the new management

Join a Housing Co-op. What Could Go Wrong?

company to take this contract over is a breach of the original contract. We find out that we will have two management companies – the old will continue to manage the building envelope project and the new company will manage the co-op including maintenance.

Should I Move?

With all the trouble I'm experiencing I'm starting to consider moving. I've put in applications at other co-ops but haven't heard anything back. It's usually a three-year wait list if co-ops are even accepting applications. I look on craigslist for places, but since I have a cat, my options are very limited. I'm now paying $900 for an 850 square foot apartment. A room in a house with 4 other people is over $1100. A studio apartment is over $1200, and a one bedroom is almost $2000! I would have to give two months' notice to the co-op on the first of the month. It just doesn't seem feasible to move. The issues I've faced so far were all fixable negating any need to move. If I can steer clear of the politics, I should be fine

Building Envelope Project

Removal of building envelope reveals that there is a cement wall between our unit and our neighbors to the left of our unit. It's a firewall that goes up the whole height of the building. That's why we never hear our neighbors on that side of the unit.

For the next two years we endure constant noise as the building envelope is removed and replaced. Our patios are also replaced, as are most of the rotting balconies. Piping in the whole building that was springing leaks is being replaced. Kitchens are upgraded. Our kitchen cabinets get upgraded even though it didn't need it. The Board member who was part of our financial team does not get his kitchen upgraded even though his cabinet doors have fallen off the hinges. This is the same member that complained about the garage fans. There is mold in their unit, but the co-op just tells them to wipe it down.

The big tree that David tried to cut down is being preserved. The building envelope contractor tells me that they had to put up a $50,000 bond to ensure the safety of the tree.

One day I come home to find that my unit door has been left unlocked. Apparently, there was some sort of inspection done or estimating done and all the doors in the co-op are unlocked.

Big Tree is Gone

Anne and I come home from a vacation to China and the beautiful tree is gone. The roots and stump near the electrical transformer box for the building have been removed.

Extra Projects, Sidewalks and Lights

Eventually the work is finishing, and life is returning to normal, but spending on projects continues. David has decided that the drain for the garage is low and should be raised. Many of us know that this is totally unnecessary. Again, these are unbudgeted items that should be brought before the membership but that just doesn't happen.

Lights outside the co-op are being replaced, again without consultation of the membership. David chose the lights and when they are turned on at night people can't sleep because the lights are so bright even with blackout curtains. A neighboring building also complains about the lights which are soccer or football field strength. The lights are slightly realigned but its now daylight outside the co-op at nighttime.

The walkway outside our building is going to be replaced. There are two small sections with cracks due to the big tree roots burrowing under the sidewalk. The tiles on the front area of the building are cracked as well. Even though only two small sections

Join a Housing Co-op. What Could Go Wrong?

need repair, but they are replacing the full one hundred feet of the walkway.

The sidewalks are removed and the tiles removed out front and the cement truck arrives. Once the cement was poured, signs were put up, but one side of the area in the front of the building was not blocked off and a delivery person walked through the wet cement to make a delivery. The area has to be dug up and poured again. The jackhammers arrive and the work begins. No warning signs are present and a senior trips and falls, breaking his wrists. Now the cement has been poured again but again the area is not taped off properly and someone in a wheelchair drives their wheelchair through the wet cement. The co-op accuses my neighbor Andy, but clearly it wasn't him because the tread marks left in the now dry cement clearly do not match the tread on his wheelchair. The area is dug up again, and fresh cement is poured and this time properly secured. The tread marks do match David's wheelchair perfectly or perhaps someone other person in the co-op or a visitor in a wheelchair has the same tire tread.

What is a problem though is that the electrical room is now flooding from the ground up. There is no report on how to deal with this.

Lindy and the Ooogly Eyes

On occasion I am either entering or leaving the garage via the elevator lobby and David and Libby's daughter Lindy makes angry faces at me. At one time I ask her what's wrong with her eyes and she stares at me and says, "You're a fucking hideous person." I tell her "May the karma that you give out come back to you ten-fold." She behaves normally for a little while but a few weeks later she comes really close to hitting me with a shopping cart as she comes out of the elevator. She pushed the cart aggressively in my direction and I have to jump out of the way to avoid getting hit. She's smart enough to scare me but not actually hit me. She repeatedly tells me I'm hideous and that I have really have no idea what I am dealing with because of her parents' connections in the co-op and how strong they are.

A few days later a neighbor gets into an argument with Lindy (David and Libby's daughter) when she almost hits her as she's crossing the path in front of the garage driveway. Lindy yells at her "You don't know who I am. My parents will make trouble for you!" A few weeks later there are rumors that she's selling her prescription drugs from her patio. The President and David knock on her door. She's told to move by the end of the day, and they change the locks on the unit. David and Gillian escort her out of the building. Her daughter is scrambling to find her a place.

Letters from the Board

A new member, Raoul arrived at the Co-op, and he's been on the board for a year now.

David and Libby are getting letters written on co-op letterhead with the signature stating it is from the co-op board. I get a letter stating that I need to be polite to contractors and treat them with the utmost respect otherwise termination could occur. The letter also accuses me of looking in David and Libby's windows. I show this to the new Board member Raoul, and he says he has no knowledge of who wrote the letter even though it came from the Board. As I am ending my conversation with Raoul another member comes to his door also complaining of a letter containing nonsensical and false accusations. Raoul tells us to ignore the letters.

The Tractor is Stolen

Members hear that the tractor that the co-op had purchased was stolen from the shed in the garage. Someone had entered, and knowing the locations of the cameras, had disabled them and made off with the tractor. A replacement was to be purchased, but again there was no involvement of the members in the allocation of funds or choosing alternatives.

The Hallway Fan Issue

It started in the middle of the day. The temperatures had dropped now that it was December. My unit's living room was next to the stairwell in which there was a heater just inside the stairwell. I started making a horrible sound that I could clearly and very loudly hear in my unit. It would overheat and eventually the thermal sensor would shut it down, but after it cooled down it would come on again. It was a horrible sound. I made a video of the noise and posted it on YouTube. Search on Youtube for "BC Co-operative Housing Stairwell Fan Noise 2017" and you can hear what I had to endure.

The noise from the fan kept me awake for two weeks and put me in the hospital from sleep deprivation and dangerously high blood pressure. I submitted a work order to the President citing my mediation agreement that defined this as an emergency, but she refused to do anything about it, putting the work-order in the co-op mailbox which was closed for at least ten days for the holidays. I got the work order back stating that it would take two months to get a replacement fan and that it could not be turned off until then.

Numerous calls and complaints to the fire dept were ignored until I reported it was clearly overheating and a hazard and that the Fire Dept would be held liable if a fire occurred. The Fire Dept finally attended and took heat readings and ordered David to immediately disconnect it. The following morning David turned it back on.

Given that I could not sleep with this thing going on, I went to his door and read the instructions. An emergency was grounds for knocking on the door and according to my mediation agreement and the assessment of the Fire Dept, this was an emergency. I knocked on his door. When he answered, I told him the fan was still on and asked him politely to turn it back off. The co-op president was in his unit visiting. All three starting yelling obscenities at me, verbally abusing me, telling me to Fuck off and move out. David came out of his apartment with his fists raised and yelling "Meet me in the stairwell, and we'll settle this like men." As I backed off, he chased me down the hall with his fists raised. I returned to my home and called the police.

Fortunately, the attending officer was the president of another co-op and knew the rules and responsibilities of the Board and advised them to disconnect it immediately and to stop threatening me. David came over and went to the basement electrical room. I could hear the door opening and closing. He turned off the fan again and then Gillian and her daughter showed up and claimed there was nothing wrong with the fan. David called an electrician, and the heater was disconnected from the other heaters.

Speaking to Board member, Raoul, he tells me that Gillian claimed there was nothing wrong with the fan and that I was crazy. I filed grievances against all three for their abusive language and behavior, but the Board never responded.

Revised Policy Manual

Gillian has rewritten the policy manual. A review of the old and new reveals that she has deleted the grievance policy and all the financial policies. The new policy manual is discussed at a general meeting but erupts in dissent when the new smoking policy is entertained. The Board thanks Gillian for retyping the old policy manual, but I remind them that I was the one who scanned it, ran it through OCR software, made any corrections and reformatted it, and had sent it to her.

Join a Housing Co-op. What Could Go Wrong?

Andy Being Evicted Again

The co-op is trying to evict Andy again because he has three cats and they claim his daughter living with him. They also accuse him of leaving some vacuum cleaners by the garbage bins. Since he's in a wheelchair, that's highly unlikely. Andy died a week later of a heart attack. Gillian's brother moves into the unit.

Eviction of Another Neighbor

My neighbor is dealing with health issues and mistakes by the management company regarding his subsidy calculation. His girlfriend is staying with him overnight occasionally to take care of him. The co-op is claiming she is living there which would affect his subsidy. He goes into the hospital and has to have his leg amputated. His girlfriend gets a knock at the door and is told she has to be out of the apartment by the end of the month, because rent has not been paid. She is told that a termination meeting was held, and no appeal was filed so he's out. She protests saying that they never received any notification. The management company was in the habit of taping important notices to doors and the notice falling off the door. The next day his girlfriend comes home to find the locks are changed and she cannot get into his apartment A few days later David and Gillian are at their door with a moving company packing up his things. They are put in storage, and he will be given the bill. He comes out of the hospital a few days later to find that he is homeless. Nobody seems to know what happened to his cat.

A New Member Upstairs

Another former co-op member moved into back in. She was constantly letting her door slam and waking us up late and early. Both Anne and I went up to talk to her. She was quite confrontational. She said "Well, it's a really heavy door" I explained that her door closing mechanism need to be replaced as

39

it was causing the door to slam really hard. Anne tried to speak to her and calm things down. I suspected that David and Libby, with whom she was good friends, had turned her against me just like they had with others. The door wasn't fixed but she did attempt to close it more softly.

A year later the member upstairs from us had moved out. She resigned from the Board and told me that she is fed up and disgusted with the politics. She gave her notice. I asked her where she was moving to, and she said she will couch surf if she has to until she finds a place. The two months have gone by, and she is much more polite to me. She talks about how messed up the co-op is and how terrible the Board is. She hasn't found a place yet. She'll have to couch surf for a while.

A new member moves in. He asked me what to do about the carpet in his bedroom because it was all bunched up in the middle. It hadn't been installed properly. I advised him to fill out a work order. Two weeks later he started getting drunk and playing loud music at 2 am. I knocked on his door to ask him to turn it down. He started yelling at me and screamed at me telling me to "fuck off and go talk to the office" He moved out at the end of the month.

A New New Member Upstairs

A new member Theresa moved in and almost immediately joined the Board. A few days after she moved in, I came home to notice water dripping from the ceiling. I knocked on her door but there was no answer. I saw David outside and told him about it. He said the cleaners were cleaning the walkway and it was probably just that. I went back into my apartment and saw more water dripping and the ceiling starting to stain. A few hours later I heard her footsteps in the apartment above and went up to see her. She opened the door and took me into the kitchen. Her whole dining floor was soaking wet. The sink drain had been plugged with a

Join a Housing Co-op. What Could Go Wrong?

stopper to do the dishes, and the tap had been dripping filling the sink. Water had overflowed all over the floor. I reported the ceiling damage, and nothing was done to repair it for a couple of months. It took multiple work orders to get it repaired.

A few months later I heard a very loud thump and a scream and moaning coming from Theresa's apartment. I called 911 to report that someone might be in distress. I went up to her door and knocked to see if she was ok. She came to her door and said everything was ok. Another person pushed past her and wearing only shorts and a bra, said "My mom pushed me" I was still on the phone with 911 and I told them the person had answered the door, and they seemed ok. They asked, "Do you still need an ambulance, fire or police?" to which I replied "No, I don't think so…" and ended the call, but her daughter said "My mom pushed me and you need to call the police." I looked at Theresa and her daughter and thought for a second or two wondering what to do. I said, "I think this is between the two of you and I feel very uncomfortable getting involved." Theresa seemed relieved. Her daughter made no further comments. I walked away.

The Start of my Demise - Noise from Electrical Room.

In the Fall of 2018, a noise started in my unit. A low-level hum that kept me awake. An engineer was called in and using sound and vibration measuring equipment confirmed there was some sort of noise. I had to resort to sleeping medication and getting alternate accommodation through Airbnb. In January I had a hernia operation and could not sleep. I ended up back at the hospital with an infection. I used sleeping medication to recover as best as I could until I could drive myself to an Airbnb to get some sleep.

The Co-op Management Company's electrician attended but he didn't seem to understand how an electrical panel could make noise. As he put a panel cover back in place the whole electrical panel vibrated and made and buzzing sound, but he failed to notice it. their electrical engineer but he did not understand anything about sound waves, asking me how a noise could go from the basement up one floor.

He was back at the building a few days later at a time when I could hear the noise, so I approached him politely to check out the panel and come hear the noise, he came into the garage but didn't go any further. A few days later, Bobby, the Management's handyman came into the unit and could hear the noise too. As we were talking the Skytrain went by and I closed the window saying that with the window closed we wouldn't hear the SkyTrain, and that it was just a fact of living near the tracks.

A few days later I got a letter from the Co-op Management stating that I was belligerent and adamant with the electrician that he check for the noise again. My conversation with Bobby the handyman was also referenced saying that I was complaining about the Skytrain noise and a host of other problems. The tone of this letter was clearly derogatory and written in a way that tried to paint me in a bad light. I suspect it was written by David and Libby.

I talk to BC Hydro, and they state that, if called, they can come in to inspect the electrical equipment. Apparently, there are some transformers at the bottom of the panel that only BC Hydro is allowed to access. The co-op management company is stating that it will take thirty days to get BC hydro to come in to check the panel but calling BC Hydro again and explaining I can't sleep because of the electrical noise, they say they can be there in 15 minutes. The electrician arrives and I ask him about the letter I got with all the accusations. He refuses to talk to me and tells me to talk to the Co-op management company office. I leave him alone. When BCHydro arrives they bring a huge wrench to tighten the connections in the panel. But the BC Hydro person says that the

Join a Housing Co-op. What Could Go Wrong?

electrical equipment is inside the building, so it is the co-op's responsibility. The co-op claims it is BC Hydro's responsibility.

A week later I talk to Bobby and mention that our conversation ended up in a letter reprimanding me and he told me that he felt he was being "thrown under the bus." He also talked about how he spotted and advertisement looking for handymen by his employer offering a higher wage than he was making. He was annoyed and unhappy and also commented that David and Libby had many friends in the co-op and that was causing problems.

Advised to Call the Emergency Line

I was advised by Raoul that the Board had arranged for an engineer to be on call who would come to investigate. With an expensive handheld acoustic and vibration measuring device the engineer confirmed that there was some sort of vibration and low frequency noise occurring. They went to the basement to try to determine the cause but were unable to do so.

A co-op volunteer attended as well. The volunteer suggested it was the ventilation system in the boiler room, but I discounted that. David came over with President Gillian and he also suggested it was the ventilation system based on a vent just outside my unit, but I reminded them that this vent went underneath the tool room, not under my unit.

Next Electrician

This noise has gone on for months now, with my sleep disturbed and my health failing and my blood pressure stuck at a very high level. Medication is not doing anything to lower it.

The electrician ended up sick and unable to do any further work, or perhaps he quit. The property management company writes to me saying they want to solve this, but they say they had no electrician at the moment and were calling around to find an electrician.

I was informed by the Co-op that an electrician would be coming by to investigate the noise. I get a knock at the door and answer. The electrician says he will not come into my unit because he is aware that there has been police involvement. I explained to him that I was the abused party and was the person who called the police because of physical and verbal threats.

He asks about the nature of the noise, and I describe it. He says he has no keys and will talk to the co-op. He calls me back later and starts talking about the politics and the police involvement again. I remind him that he brought up this topic. I remind him that he has been misguided by what has transpired. He hangs up and never returns.

Strange Man in my Unit

One day I came home from work in the middle of the afternoon. I entered my unit and as I put my briefcase down a strange man in overalls came out of my bedroom. Startled I demanded "Who are you and who let you into my apartment. He told me he was an electrician contracted by the Co-op management company to investigate an electrical issue. I asked him how he got into my unit, and he replied that a courier delivered a set of master keys to him outside the building. I told him that the electrical issue was in the electrical room and not in my unit. He asked how he could get into the electrical room and told him he needed to use his master keys. I showed him the electrical room, and he said this issue was beyond his capabilities and said that he couldn't do anything. He tried to get me to take the master keys, but I refused knowing that I'd be accused of going into other people's units. He had to wait for two hours outside the building for a courier to come

Join a Housing Co-op. What Could Go Wrong?

pick up the keys. The electrician does note that there is significant elevator noise in my unit.

I talked to Board member Raoul who told me that I was wasting all the co-ops management hours, but I explained that the management company had emailed me saying that they were spending a lot of time finding an electrician. I explained that the management company was likely billing them for time spent to find an electrician rather than doing actual co-op work. The management company had claimed in presentations that they always had a full roster of contractors. I complained about the electrician coming into my unit unescorted and Raoul said that someone had let him in. Anne and I were divorced, and she had moved out so I told him I lived alone now that Anne had moved out and the only person who could have let me in was my cat. He asked me for a copy of that email, and I left it taped to his mailbox instead of bothering him by knocking on his door. He then later accused me of harassing him and committing a felony by leaving the copy of the email taped to his mailbox.

The Management Company's solution to the electrical issue was to place rubber insulation on the panels. It made no difference.

Severe Insomnia, High Blood Pressure and a Hernia

Over the next few months, I had severe insomnia because of the noise. In the fall I attempted to sleep in my car. I started booking Airbnb accommodations to get sleep. I January 2019 I needed a hernia operation and when I came home from the hospital I could not sleep again from the noise. I ended up with an infection. I took sleeping pills to get some rest and as soon as I could drive, I booked myself into an Airbnb for three nights to get some sleep.

Then the management company was now claiming there was no noise. I replied back to them that the noise had already been confirmed by one engineer and a co-op maintenance volunteer.

Any attempts to ask any Board members about the issue were met with a stern "no".

Call to the Bylaw Officers

One evening when the noise was quite bothersome, I called the city bylaw line who in turn told me to call the RCMP, who in turn told me to call the City By law enforcement. The bylaw enforcement people said that they only deal with complaints at the property line. Since the noise was in the building, there was nothing they could do.

Election Chaos

Elections are about to occur, but even the Management Company says in a meeting that they can't make heads or tails of which Board members have reached their term limit. I had obtained the filings of Board member changes and discover that term limits have not been respected. I present the information to the Board and the Management company. I'm away on vacation when the election occurs and again the term limits aren't respected, nor are positions put up for election that should be available. One member who wasn't in attendance at the AGM is nominated and added to the board which is against the rules. Within a few days she resigns from the Board. The Board appointed a replacement without any nomination or election process.

Definitely an Electrical Problem!

One evening in the cold of winter the noise from below my unit got very loud. I called the volunteer to help me and he came over. He also brought the President Raoul along. We all go into the electrical room to see what is going on. The electrical panel is

Join a Housing Co-op. What Could Go Wrong?

making a very loud hum. Whenever the elevator compressor kicks in a section of the panel makes a very loud bang! Clearly there is something wrong with the panel. The President promises to get this fixed. A few weeks later he assures me it has been fixed. The banging noise has stopped but the hum is still present.

New President Harasses Me?

On a sunny summer Sunday of a long weekend, I'm awoken at exactly 9:01 am an extremely loud gas-powered lawn trimmer being used right outside my bedroom window. I had been looking forward to a good night's sleep, but the President of the Co-op, Raoul, was outside my window making the noise. He shut it off a few minutes later. I told him, while this might be legal because the bylaw states no use until after 9 am on Sundays, it is not helpful because I was trying to sleep in. He looked really embarrassed but did not apologize. He didn't say anything.

Agency Mocks Me

Since I now had proof that there was an issue with the electrical system in the building, I approached the government offices of Agency, which managed its co-op contracts. I reported the issue to them for inclusion in their report of hazards and liabilities regarding their assets. This had no effect other than to be told not to contact the employee. Since things were really going bad at the co-op, I requested that CMHC appoint a board as per the conditions of their contract which I pointed out in my letter to them and the violations of the contract. The CMHC Agency employee responded with a terse email stating "Nice Try!". I forwarded that email to their legal counsel and a few days later received a reply and apology from the employee. A month later the co-op refinanced the CMHC mortgage so the Agency and CMHC were now longer involved.

Mark Linden O'Meara

Electrical Conduit From Transformer To Building Damaged?

I spoke with an electrical contractor who had originally done work on the building. He was able to pull up the plans for the building and state that the conduit going from the outside transformer to the building was likely damaged and this could be the cause of the noise and certainly the cause of ground water seeping into the electrical room. I wrote a letter to the Board outlining this possibility but got no response other than a comment "Now he thinks it's the transformer."

Trying to Talk to Board Members

Angela (the member who flooded her unit with sewage from cat litter) and I have always been on good terms, saying hello to each other. She is now on the Board. Since we rarely have meetings, and my work orders and letters are being ignored regarding the noise in my unit, I politely ask Angela if she can help. She says that all the Board members have been instructed not to talk to me. I asked her who issued this notice, but she says she can't tell me. I wish her a good day and walk away. Multiple websites and agencies state on their website to contact the CHF-BC if you have an issue in your co-op but the CHF-BC only tells you to talk to your Board. Obviously, that's not working in this case.

Sleeping in a Tent on My Patio

The noise continued… It's the rainy fall season now and the electrical load has increased with people running their electrical heat. The noise continues and I am unable to sleep in my unit due to the hum. I had run out of funds to stay at an Airbnb. I set up a large tent on my patio, equipped it with an air mattress and blankets and plugged in a heater to keep me warm from the cold. I used silicon air plugs to try to drown out the Skytrain noise. I did this for about two weeks. I also tried to sleep in my car but the dust in the garage was a problem due to dust and allergies and the overhead lights kept me awake. Being six feet tall also meant that I had to try to sleep at an awkward angle. I reverted back to the tent after a few nights, but then came a snowstorm, and the melting snow flooded the tent and my blankets. I gave up on the tent idea.

False Information to The Board

Since I was getting no response from the Management Company, I posted a request on their Facebook page to please contact me to help resolve this noise issue. The owner of the Management Company replied with a comment that there was no noise and that I had been offered two different units to move to but had refused these. I politely corrected this misinformation. Realizing that this avenue of communication was not going to get anything resolved, I deleted the posts.

Having requested Board minutes, I discovered that former President Gillian had been invited to a Board meeting to provide information about me. Her comments to the Board, recorded in the Board minutes totally distorted the mediation process. She wasn't present during the mediation meetings. She falsely claimed the mediation efforts were to deal with allegations that I wasn't following the work order process. She claimed I had been offered two different units to move to. This was totally false, but once a lie is started it's very hard to change people's opinions.

I sent a Cease-and-Desist letter to the Board and Gillian stating that Gillian was not involved in the mediation, that the information she presented was incorrect, and advising them to stop the breach of my mediation agreement that included no gossiping.

I file grievances against David, Libby, Theresa and Gillian for their abusive behavior. I also request mediation. All of these are ignored.

Acoustic Engineer Number Two

Finally, the Board agreed to bring in a second Acoustic Engineering company. Despite the noise happening at night, the co-op arranged for a noise measurement during the daytime. The Acoustic Engineer showed up at 9:30 am as a compromise. They advised me they were there to measure the elevator noise. I advised them that was incorrect, that there was another noise that needed to be investigated - a low-level hum. They said they were not instructed to investigate anything other than the elevator noise. The contractor made a few phone calls and announced that they would measure the elevator noise and come back a second time to measure any other noises. A week passed before they returned.

Elevator Noise Resolution

The Acoustic Engineer notes that there is significant noise from the elevator. I tell him that I've been told there is nothing they can do to fix it. He states that is incorrect and starts working with the elevator maintenance company to resolve it. The noise diminishes to 10% of what it was before and approximately what it was like when I moved in.

Acoustic Engineer Second Visit

The Acoustic Engineer returns a second time to do the work that the Management Company did not properly request on the work order.

They shut off all equipment in the boiler room and garage fans etc and can confirm there is a hum. The Acoustic Engineer asks me if I can hear it. I reply that I'm so exhausted from lack of sleep that I think I can hear it but I'm no longer certain. He tells me this is a common effect of being exposed to ongoing low-level sounds. He confirms that he can hear it. I'm to wait for the report to be sent to the Board.

Join a Housing Co-op. What Could Go Wrong?

In the meantime, despite being polite, I received a letter from the co-op stating that "derogatory comments about concierges, management or contractors would not be tolerated." I replied back asking what comments were of concern and got no reply.

Acoustic Report Confirms Noise

The report by the Acoustic contractor was sent to the Board by the Acoustic contractor.

It described three confirmed sources of noise.

- Boiler room fan
- Elevator
- Multiple harmonics from the "transformer" audible in my unit.

The report also confirmed that the Acoustic Engineer could hear a very audible hum in the unit and confirmed with me that it was the noise I was hearing. In the report the Acoustic Engineer stated that these noises could only be coming from the transformer. I was confused because the transformer for the building was located on the lawn about fifty feet from the building. I called him to clarify, and he stated that he meant the electrical panel and equipment underneath my unit. He said he would notify the co-op to clarify this.

Excerpt from Acoustic Report:

> "With both the exhaust fan and fresh air supply fan deactivated, the ambient noise spectrum fell below the threshold of hearing. Nevertheless, a hum was still audible to the occupant of Unit 106 and was confirmed to be present by the report author. In Figure 3, tonal components are present at 60Hz, 120Hz and 240Hz.

The transformer is the only piece of mechanical or electrical equipment in continuous operation that could produce these tonal components. Under increased load, the transformer would likely produce higher levels of vibration and noise.

Transformer vibration and noise can be attenuated by mounting the transformer on vibration isolators and ensuring that the connections between the bus-ways and transformers are sufficiently flexible.

We recommend a joint inspection with the transformer engineer to determine whether the transformer has been isolated, and if so whether the isolation is compromised in any way. We can then potentially work with the transformer engineer to isolate the unit or rectify any isolation faults.

Management Company Report Error

Despite the clear indication by the Acoustic Company that there is electrical noise, the management company does not include that information nor the recommendations to resolve it in their report to the Board. I get a letter from the Board:

> Re: LETTER OF OUTCOME - response to your letter and outcome of BAP acoustical report
>
> Dear Mark O'MEARA,
>
> The board received your correspondence through the package received by drop box and sent to management company. This is the following outcome from the [Acoustic Engineer] Acoustical Report:
>
> 1. Identified noise sources were from two sources:
>   1.1. Elevator/machine room -

Join a Housing Co-op. What Could Go Wrong?

        recommendations were put forth to the board on how to minimize the noise and the management company has given those recommendations to West Coast Elevator company who does the maintenance on the elevator to order the parts (which will take up to 6 to 8 weeks to get in) and begin the installation of the parts.

  1.2. Boiler room fan - recommendations were put forth to the board to change how the fan is mounted to prevent the vibrations from the fan to transfer through the concrete. The management company has generated a work order for Cityscape to come in and source out the parts and system to make this change over and should be commencing within the next 2 weeks the work should be done.

2. The board is closing this upon completion of those two items being repaired and modified as per the suggestion put forth by SAP Acoustical.

The board now considers this to be closed upon completion of the work and will not entertain any further complaints or letters upon this subject.

    If you have further question, please contact Management Company or email:

Thank you,

    On behalf of the board of directors

    Clearly the management company and the board missed the main issue in the report. The recommended joint inspection never happened.

Another Consultant

I also learned from the Board minutes that another consultant had been hired to assess noise but without my knowledge or involvement. I requested a copy of the report. The report assessed noise I the basement but not in my unit. I called the consultant and spoke with him. He was very polite and helpful. He told me he was unaware of any noise in my unit, nor was he aware of the Acoustic Engineer's report. He had only been asked to assess the noise in the basement.

Filing a Case with The Civil Resolution Tribunal

I'm getting nowhere with the Board and have exhausted all avenues of help. I learned that the Civil Resolution Tribunal was now willing to hear cases with Housing Co-operatives. I now finally had access to the justice system with this change. Small claims court would not have worked because Small Claims court could not issue directives or orders to remedy an issue.

I gathered all my documents and filed a case with the Civil Resolution Tribunal. Despite this being an urgent issue, it would take weeks to get this resolved.

The Management Company responded to my complaint, in violation of the CRT rules that a representative of the co-op must be the respondent. The CRT issues an official order listing the items we agreed to.

I had to file an official complaint. This delayed the process by a couple of weeks. Management Company states they will represent the co-op at the CRT meeting. This is in violation of the CRT rules that state that the representative must be a member of the co-op. I file a request to remove the Management Company, but this will take a few weeks to resolve.

Join a Housing Co-op. What Could Go Wrong?

CRT Meeting

Theresa, the board member upstairs agreed to represent the co-op. A mediator was appointed and he gathered documents and responses from both sides of the dispute. She stated that the co-op was aware of the electrical room problems and that it was an unrepairable situation. She said that she wasn't bothered by noise and suggested we switch apartments, without any inspection, and that the co-op would agree to reimbursing me for the Airbnb expenses. She also stated emphatically that there was no noise in her unit at all. I repeatedly asked her this question.

The CRT issues an official order listing the items we agreed to as follows:

> This order is in full and final settlement of this dispute.
>
> I order that:
>
> On April 15, 2020, or prior to April 15, 2020 on a date mutually agreed in writing by bath parties, the applicant remit occupancy of unit #XXX, and take occupancy of unit #YYY.
>
> The respondent ensure that unit #YYY is vacant such that the applicant can occupy the unit as required in term 1 of this order.
>
> This order does net in way affect the applicant's membership in the coop.
>
> Within 4 business days of the date this order is signed and distributed to parties by the CRT, the respondent pay to the applicant $2,725.00. as noted in term 5 of this agreement.

The sum of $1,225.00 be paid to the applicant by cheque delivered by hand to the applicant by the respondent, and $1,500.00 be remitted directly to the co-op and without being paid to the applicant, for the applicant's membership top-up.

Neither the applicant's current unit #XXX nor unit #YYY require further inspection prior to the change in occupancy noted on term 1 of this agreement.

Signed by CRT Officers AAA and BBB

After the CRT Meeting

Later that week we agreed on a date to move, which would be March 28th. I began tidying up and started to pack. With experience as a mover back in my university days, I knew that this type of move, with two people switching units in the same building, was a challenging one to pull off. I suggested we use the courtyard as a staging area. We could move one room of my unit to the staging area, the she could move her room into my unit, and then proceed with the same process with the living room, dining room, and storage.

I arranged for a friend to monitor the staging area so that our belongings would not be stolen. At one time Anne had left a pair of running shoes in the courtyard to dry and twenty minutes later they were stolen. I didn't want any of our belongings to be stolen. I purchase a canopy tent to keep our things dry. It came with a wrap around cover so the only access would be from the front of the tent. I arranged for movers as well.

The co-op issued a cheque, as per the CRT order, to cover my Airbnb costs less the increase in the share deposit which will be placed on my share account for the new unit.

Join a Housing Co-op. What Could Go Wrong?

With the moving date approaching, for the next two weeks I stayed in an Airbnb so I can sleep. I start packing, and although I don't have to, I start making minor touch up repairs to my apartment, and replace some of the laminate flooring boards that have slight damage from wear and tear.

Friendly Inspection of Units.

A few friends warn me that I should go up and check her unit to make sure everything was ok. Theresa agreed to this. A week later we visited each other's units. She mentioned that her unit was scheduled for renovations of the kitchen. This was something I was unaware of. Secondly, the noise complaint of her stomping had been addressed with carpet but only on certain areas with really obtuse angles. The design of this would give most people vertigo with the angles used.

But much more problematic was the fact that I could hear the same noise in her bedroom. The noise from the transformer could be travelling up the cement firewall in the bedroom. The electrical equipment in the basement was attached to this firewall. I raised this issue with her and she replied that "I'm half deaf so I wouldn't hear it." I also noticed her ceiling fan spinning in the dining area. It was very wobbly and out of balance.

COVID Hits

And so, the move was planned for the 28th. But on March 23rd Covid broke out and everything went into lockdown. We were told by the media that we had to socially distance. My classes were moved online, stores closed, and directives were issued by the provincial and federal government to socially isolate. The co-op office was closed. There was no one available to re-key the locks as are standard practice when someone moves. Theresa's daughter might still have a key to my new unit.

I had been exposed to Covid at work. A fellow employee's wife had contracted it, and he advised us in an email that he had been exposed. I had met him a few times in the hallway. I'm not sure if it is legal for the movers to continue working. From the layout of the building, there is no way that I can move and practice social distancing. I reach out to the CRT but they had no guidance. The courts are closed so I can't file the order in either provincial or supreme courts to make it official.

I email Theresa and advise her that we need to postpone the move due to the Covid outbreak and could we please discuss the matter.

This is the email I sent:

> Tuesday, March 24, 2020 10:17 AM
>
> Cancellation of Move this Saturday
>
> I would like to advise you that due to COVID-19, it is my fiduciary duty to practice social distancing. As a result, it is necessary to call off the move for this Saturday.
>
> I viewed unit YYY and found that the same noise level is present in the bedroom. I was previously advised that there was no noise in the unit at all, which was incorrect. The core issue of the CRT Tribunal proceedings has not been resolved. Therefore, 1 don't think we can proceed with the move on the 28th.
>
> 1 will be more than happy to hear back from you as to how we can resolve this.
>
> There is still a need to resolve this vibration issue coming from the transformer below me. 1 am unable to

Join a Housing Co-op. What Could Go Wrong?

sleep in unit XXX and would have experienced the same issue in YYY.

Please call BC Hydro to come in and investigate the equipment that they have in the bottom portion of the distribution panel or contact the equipment manufacturer as recommended by Acoustics Engineer (item 4-e in their report).

Thank you,

A few days letter I get a strongly worded letter. The Co-op claimed that based on the language in my letter I was in default of the CRT order and the co-op is demanding repayment of the money they paid me in respect of the order otherwise the account will be sent to a collections agency which would ruin my credit rating.

This is the letter I received.

> March 25, 2020
> Re: CANCELLATION OF MOVE email from you March 24th
>
> Dear Mark O'MEARA,
>
> We write with respect to your email advice of March 24, 2020 that you detect noise in unit 2- YYY and in particular your statement that:
>
>> "I viewed unit YYY and found that the same noise level is present in the bedroom due. I was previously advised that there was no noise in the unit at all, which was incorrect. The core issue of the CRT Tribunal proceedings has not

been resolved. "

The final order of the Tribunal was entered into "...in full and final settlement of this dispute". You approved this order and it was then certified. You accepted the monetary settlement funds. You accepted the unit which was offered to you. Theresa maintains that she has detected no untoward noise in her unit during the past four years of her tenancy.

Despite the above, you continue to raise the subject of the dispute that has been fully adjudicated. Your decision to default has caused unnecessary stress to Theresa, who is at present half packed to move on schedule and has contacted various service providers of her contemplated new address as of March 28th. This is unacceptable.

The Board Members consider the language in your email as your default of the consent order. As such, we advise as follows:

1. You will return the funds given to you ($1,225 + $125 CRT filing fees) as per the order <u>forthwith</u>, failing which we have instructions to commence collection proceedings against you.
2. The amount of $1,500 placed in share purchase on your behalf will be returned to the membership.
3. Since you have defaulted, Ms. Theresa has no faith you are willing to go through the process of switching units. She has, understandably, no confidence that you will honor your commitment should a new move date be discussed. She has gone through time, money and trouble to honor her commitment to no avail.

Join a Housing Co-op. What Could Go Wrong?

4   Your name will be placed on an internal wait list for the next available one-bedroom apartment in Building 2. Should you refuse the next available unit, your name will be removed to the bottom of the waiting list.
5   It is the position of the Board Members that all reasonable action has been taken with respect to your noise issues over the past six or more months and they are no longer prepared to expend more time or money these items.
6   Going forward, Management Company has been instructed to disregard any correspondence from you that involves the alleged noise in your current unit. This directive is directly related to the time and money necessary to continue to deal with a member issue that has been adjudicated.
7   You are directed to communicate all matters regarding your unit at [redacted] only through the normal Management Company email address: [redacted]. Do not leave messages or communicate with current or former Board Members about this matter.
8   Should you attempt to file another dispute about your personal noise issues, be aware that we will vigorously object to your right to relitigate these issues and request reimbursement of the costs to do so.

Thank you,

On behalf of the board of Directors of Co-op and Management Company

So Much for Discussion

The letter states that I'll be put at the top of the wait list for another unit. I repay the money to the co-op and write "Paid under duress" on the cheque. If I don't pay this money they might report me to the Credit Bureau instantly destroying my credit rating. There is now no point in sending letters to the office, as the management company has been advised to ignore all correspondence. I contact the CRT Office for guidance regarding Covid regarding an order that had specific dates and also regarding misinformation presented in my mediation meeting. The CRT has nothing to say other than to talk to a lawyer. They are unwilling to provide any help. They state that filing deadlines have been extended but orders cannot be changed.

Victim Services Referral

A co-op volunteer has been trying to help me with the noise. At a time when I could hear the noise he came over. He took me to the electrical room, and we found that the equipment was completely quiet. The repair of the switch seemed to have fixed the issue. But there was still a noise coming from somewhere. The noise could be heard in my unit, in the stairwell, and on the third floor, which would be Theresa's ceiling. It seemed to be coming from the second-floor ceiling but with my knowledge of acoustics I understand that it could be coming from anywhere.

I knocked on Theresa's door and politely asked her if she could turn off her ceiling fan to verify if that was the cause. She said "No! I'm fed up with this! I returned to my unit.

With the noise going fully, I asked the co-op volunteer to help me. He came over and could confirm there was some sort of humming noise that could be heard in my unit and in the area around the stairwell area. He politely asked Theresa to turn off her improperly installed wobbly ceiling fan for a few seconds to see if that was the source of the noise. Again, she refused.

I called the City of Burnaby to file a noise complaint. Again, they referred me to the RCMP. An officer attended and I explained

Join a Housing Co-op. What Could Go Wrong?

the history. The officer spoke to Theresa. Based on the officer's interaction with Theresa, the officer referred me to Victim Services. Victim Services told me the only thing they could suggest was to go sleep in a homeless shelter.

Attempt to File the CRT Order in Courts

The CRT order I have is unenforceable until I file it in the courts which are now closed because of Covid. I am in contact with the courts by phone and they say I can file online. I try to file online but I need a case number. I can only get a case number by coming into a court, but the courts are closed.

The courts are moving to an online filing system, and I'm told that I can file the CRT order. I try, but the CRT order I have is rejected by the court system saying the file is password protected. I get through to the CRT help desk and they insist the file is not password protected. If I try to print the CRT order as a PDF it asks for a password. I relay this information to the CRT who again insist there is no password. I'm back and forth with the CRT. Eventually a clerk calls me back and says, "I'm so sorry, you need help with this, and we have let you down." She tries to help but finally gives up saying, "Yes, it is password protected so that the document cannot be altered. You will have to wait until the courts open."

A Plea for Help

I'm completely exhausted and frustrated that the CRT will not modify the order based on the implications of Covid and the new information I have, and the misinformation presented in the meeting.

I speak to a few friends, and they all advise me that I need an advocate to help me. One friend even quotes Einstein saying "Mark, you can't solve this on the level of consciousness that created it. You need an advocate."

Mark Linden O'Meara

At their suggestion, I write a letter to anyone who might be able to help.

Here is the letter I sent: (names removed)

Federal Housing MP
Local BC-MLA
BC Minister for Municipal Affairs and Housing
Federal Cabinet MP responsible for CMHC
BC Deputy Minister for Housing
Contract Manager Agency.coop
President CMHC

I have a severe housing and health issues. I need immediate assistance.

I live at XXXX Housing Co-op, a great multicultural community, with great neighbors, but I need help with a severe co-op issue that is severely impacting my health and causing financial distress. I am hoping someone can intervene to sort this issue out.

I am unable to sleep in my unit due to vibration and noise coming from the electrical distribution box below my unit. This issue has been going on for approximately 14 months but is now severe. I have had to take time off work. I have been using up my savings and salary to stay in Airbnb's to try to sleep. I can not sleep in my apartment. The co-op refuses to repair the issue.

The Co-op is in breach of its occupancy agreement – duty to repair, and in breach of my right to quiet enjoyment.

Join a Housing Co-op. What Could Go Wrong?

As a result of sleep deprivation and stress, I have developed an adrenal hormone illness, and my blood pressure is 177/98, even though I am on strong blood pressure medicine. I am experiencing minor chest pains and heart palpitations. I now have an irregular ECG. I am exhausted from lack of sleep. I have provided numerous doctors notes in the last year to try to get the co-op to repair this issue.

I have a previous mediation agreement with the co-op that states that an emergency is defined as an issue that affects a member's health. The Co-op is ignoring this mediation agreement.

I've been in touch with the Ministry of Municipal Affairs and Housing, who are well aware of issues at this Co-op. The Ministry so far has been helpful, referring me to Court Services, who are only able to provide a web link to seeking an emergency Supreme Court Hearing. To apply, I will need a lawyer to assist me, but having used all my savings for places to stay, I am unable to afford legal advice, nor do I qualify for legal assistance.

On Saturday March 29, I involved the RCMP (Report BU-20-XXXX), who are attempting to refer me to "victim services" because this is a case where I need an advocate to help me, but it is unclear if they will be able to help.

The co-op hired Management Company, an unlicensed Property Management Company, to manage the affairs and maintenance of the co-op. Management Company has shown complete incompetence in trying to diagnose and effect repairs.

The Co-op and [The Management Company] now claim the electrical distribution box is 'unrepairable." Despite numerous requests, [Management Company] and the Co-op have not provided any evidence that they have brought in any electrical engineer to determine the cause of the vibration and noise coming from the distribution box, let alone any evidence it is unrepairable.

Last year, CMHC's Agency.coop advised me that the Electrical Distribution Box issue was noted on the Co-op's Annual Risk Assessment Report.

Someone has directed all Board members to not talk to me about this issue. Board members refuse to tell me who gave this directive.

I have unsuccessfully gone to the Civil Resolution Tribunal. I negotiated what I thought was an agreeable settlement due to statements made by the co-op. These statements have now been proven false. In the negotiations, the Co-op representative offered to switch units with me. Hers is directly above mine. She made representation that there was no noise in her unit. Upon the advice of a number of friends, I viewed her unit and found the noise to be present in her bedroom wall which is the same wall that the electrical distribution box is attached to in the basement. She has advised me she is "half-deaf" , therefore she was in no position to make the claims she made, which I relied on in my CRT negotiations.

Section 92 of the Civil Resolution Tribunal Act prohibits parties from providing false or misleading evidence or other information in a tribunal proceeding,

Join a Housing Co-op. What Could Go Wrong?

however the CRT doesn't have authority to investigate or prosecute offences; the provision in the Civil Resolution Tribunal Act is there for the Crown or citizens to use in the event they have the will to pursue it.

Since the move would solve nothing, and due to my fiduciary duty to practice social distancing due to COVID19, I postponed the move and asked for further discussion. The Co-op Board responded with a demand for the return of money I received as part of the CRT agreement to fund alternate accommodations until the move could occur. They demanded immediate repayment, and if I failed to comply immediately, they would send the account directly to collections. I have given the co-op a cheque for $1350, leaving me with my bank account almost empty.

The Co-op Board has advised Management Company to ignore all further correspondence from me on this issue. Board members will not talk to me about this issue. We rarely have co-op meetings.

I have contacted all the agencies below. They are all stating they are unable to help me:

- Civil Resolution Tribunal – even if there was misrepresentation and acting in bad faith, the CRT can not re-open a case.
- City of Burnaby – no maintenance bylaw, noise bylaw is not applicable to inside a building.
- Technical Safety BC – Referred me to City of Burnaby.
- BC Hydro – they state all equipment in the building is the responsibility of the Co-op.

- CMHC and Agency – state they have no mandate to get involved.
- BC Housing – although they provide funding to the Co-op they state they do not get involved in Co-op issues.
- CHF-BC – do not get involved in governance issues.
- Residential Tenancy – does not deal with Co-ops.
- Better Business Bureau – does not accept complaints about co-ops. Can not file complaint against a third party.
- RECBC – legislation requires licensing of all Property Management companies for Strata's and Tenant situations, but a loophole in the legislation allows companies like Management Company to be unlicensed and unregistered if only providing services to Co-ops.

The Co-op is in breach of its occupancy agreement – duty to repair, and in breach of my right to quiet enjoyment. It appears there is no government agency that overseas co-ops. That needs to change.

I desperately need help with this issue.

Regards

Mark O'Meara

No one replied…

Covid Restrictions Lifted – Request to Honor CRT Order

Covid restrictions are being lifted. Businesses are opening up again. I send a message to Theresa asking her to honor the CRT

Join a Housing Co-op. What Could Go Wrong?

order and proceed with the move. I get no reply. I send another email to her asking her to honor the CRT Order, but again get no reply.

Balcony Conversation Overheard by Theresa

It was now early June. I was on my balcony and talking to another member about filing a new CRT complaint for all the breaches of the Associations Act by the co-op. I had been advised to file another CRT case to rehear the noise issue. I could hear Theresa shuffling around on her balcony above me. She overheard my plans.

Elevator Noise is Back

The elevator noise which had diminished after the work by the Acoustic Engineer has returned full on. Whatever adjustments that were made have been reversed. The noise in my unit continues. I can also hear a hum on the third floor which would be Theresa's ceiling. It could be coming from anywhere.

Another New Neighbor Across the Hall

Despite supposedly being put on the top of the waiting list for a one bedroom, the one bedroom apartment across the hall becomes available but it is not offered to me.

A new neighbor moved in next to me. I said hello to her and welcomed her to the co-op. A day or two later her smoke detector went off while she was not home. When I saw her in the hallway I mentioned it to her.

Again, I called the city bylaw office and again they told me to call the police. The police attended and based on her behavior said there was nothing they could do. However, the police officer advised me that Theresa had told them I was harassing my new neighbor. I explained that all I did was say hello and let her know her smoke detector had gone off.

69

The neighbor tells me she is just temporarily in that unit, and she will be moving to another two bedroom unit down the hall as soon as it becomes available. Again, despite being at the top of the list according to the letter from the co-op there is no offer of a move.

CRT Complaints #2 and #3

The Co-op is doing nothing about the noise. The advice I receive is to file another complaint with the CRT to get the matter reviewed and a new agreement issued based on the new information. I file two separate complaints – one for the noise and one for the issues at the co-op.

I request the following to remedy the gap in what the rules and laws state and and how the Co-op Board is behaving.

- An Order that financial updates be presented to members at each meeting in accordance with our official policy manual and principles of transparency.
- An Order to the Co-op Board that Chargebacks must be approved by the board at a board meeting and recorded in the minutes.
- An Order to the Board that the AGM agenda should include a "call for items" According to the act, an agenda topic can be added if the requirements of the Act are met.
- An Order to the Board that the topic and resolution of "In Camera" sessions be recorded as per the act.
- An order to the Board that the unapproved policy manual being distributed be recalled and the official policy dated 2000 and approved modifications be distributed and followed.
- An order that complaints regarding David, Libby, and Gillian be processed in accordance with the rules and occupancy agreement regarding threats of violence.

Join a Housing Co-op. What Could Go Wrong?

- An order that the Board be directed to ignore all comments by Gillian in Meeting of Jan 2019 and amend minutes to remove false statements.
- Cease and desist orders to be issued to David, Libby and Gillian, and all Board members to restrict gossip as per mediation agreement and recent correspondence within the Board.
- An order to the Board to manage the co-op instead of delegation of duties to Management Company Management, which is a violation of the act.
- An order to the Board that Final Financial statements be distributed to members in advance of the AGM in accordance with the Act and rules and regulations of the Co-op.
- An Order to the Board that term limits be respected and that staggered elections be maintained with regard to the Act.
- An order to the board to follow the official current policy manual practice of presenting three quotes to the membership for of any expenses over $3000.
- An Order to the Board that rules and current and official policies be distributed to all members and applied equally to all members.
- An Order to the Board to meet is legal obligation to file change of directors and annual report with the BC registry services.
- An order to the Board that as per the Act, meetings be chaired by President or VP or member and that non-members i.e. the Management Company not chair meetings or be present without a motion/vote.

- An Order that Special Resolutions, especially with regard to elections must be presented to the membership in accordance with the Act, Rules and Policies.

The CRT speaks with the Co-op President. Both complaints are merged into one and put on hold pending the termination of my membership. The Co-op is claiming that the noise issue has already been heard and that termination of my membership would remove my right to proceed with the complaints.

Trying to Enforce CRT Order Leads to Termination

As previously mentioned above, when Covid restrictions were lifted in June 2020 I emailed Theresa to request that she honor the court order and suggest a move date. I got no reply, but a package was delivered to my door advising me that my membership was being terminated. Theresa had begun a campaign against me to evict me.

I had to appear before the Board in 7 days. I received the notice on a Friday afternoon before a long weekend. I essentially had 4 business days to find a lawyer and develop a response. I spent the next few days preparing a response and trying to find a lawyer. I found a lawyer but all he offered to do was sit with me at the meeting. He offered no legal advice, opinion, nor did he warn the board about human rights violations they were committing. He also failed to tell me to write "without prejudice" on my submission so that it could not be used against me. This cost me $1500.

Response and presentation at the Board meeting regarding my Termination Meeting

- Conflict of Interest: Board Members Theresa, Raoul, and Vivian are biased and in conflict of interest and must exclude themselves from vote.

Join a Housing Co-op. What Could Go Wrong?

- I have requested a copy of the official policy manual but only received every 2nd page. They have sent me a new policy manual that was never approved by the membership. This was needed to prepare my case.

Preamble

- This has been extremely frustrating for both of us.
- 18 months and we have no resolution
- I'm hear to clarify the issues raised but I'm hear to listen
- We need to work together to resolve this.
- Good communication means asking questions and listening.

"The most courageous people to me are those who are willing to look at themselves and admit they have a mindset that is part of the problem and knowing it can be changed for the better. That includes me. "

All problems started with conflict David when I told him to stop knocking on my door. And when Victor, Roger, I and Andy and I researched financial transactions and reported irregularities to the Board. Then I was accused of:

- o Taking liberties with the tool room turning it into a gym -false
- o A snake in the grass
- o Offered multiple units and turned them down.
- o Telling contractors to be careful of him because there's been police involvement
- o Made a mess in the gardening room
- o Claiming I was looking into their windows. No one on Board knew who wrote that letter.

Thats's just what I've heard, I'm sure there's much more.

Grievances against the David, Libby and Gillian for abusive behavior, homophobic slurs, being yelled at and sworn at, a death threat, and repeated threats of violence have never been followed up by the Co-op.

Addressing Claims:

- Co-op is in breach of Occupancy Agreement, Right to Quiet Enjoyment
- The Board's lack of proper action on the noise issue is the cause of all of this issue before us.
- Principles of Natural Justice are not being followed. I am not being heard, and information needed such as official Policy manual is not being provided to me.
- Management Company Management is a third party and Co-op has no jurisdiction over alleged comments made about a 3rd party and not a member of the co-op. If Management Company has an issue with me they need to approach me about this without the involvement of the co-op. They are being sued by other co-ops and there are numerous complaints about Management Company from the membership.

- Issues with Theresa and Raoul are member to member and not the jurisdiction of the Board. Advice to other members is to try to resolve with other member. I expect the same treatment., Theresa and Raoul should file grievances.
- From Official Policy Manual:

Join a Housing Co-op. What Could Go Wrong?

Disputes

62. Any dispute arising out of the affairs of the Association, between a member thereof, or any person aggrieved who has for not more than six (6) months ceased to be a member, or any person claiming through such member or person aggrieved, or claiming under the Rules, and the Association or a Director thereof, shall be referred to a committee of three (3) members of the Association. The President and the member or other person aggrieved shall each nominate one (1) member, and the third shall be chosen by the two (2) so nominated. The decision of the committee shall be final and binding on all parties and may be enforced on application to a County Court.

Writing a letter to your MLA about a valid concern asking for help is not "conduct detrimental to the co-op"
- No indication of what phrases in the letters are "conduct detrimental to the Co-op" and requests for such answers have not been responded to.
- There is no direction from the Police to not talk to Board members nor any direction to not talk to anyone in the co-op. This wrong information being spread by Theresa.
- Mediation Agreement is being ignored and all further requests for mediation have been ignored.
- Equal treatment of Members: Others members have yelled at me, threatened me with physical violence, and hurled homophobic insults and a death threat. These actions have been ignored. despite filing grievances.
- I have requested Mediation at least three times in the last two years and not received any response to my requests.
- Regarding CRO, Public Health Emergency takes precedence over CRO.

Enforcement of CRO Creates Bias of Board member and serious legal problem for co-op.

- I have been unable to file the CRO in court to enforce because courts are closed. Courts will open for filing on Monday July 13th.
- If I do proceed, and terminated, and then enforcement occurs, MS Theresa will have to vacate her unit. If my unit (106) is occupied by someone else after my termination, she will be homeless.
- CRO states that "This order does not in any way affect the applicant's membership on the co-op"
- Theresa must not participate in this vote due to conflict of interest and bias.

Regarding Contact with Board and Obtaining Names and Addresses

Board member information (names and unit numbers was provided to me by Management Company Management and is a public document with BC Registries. Notices left on door are in accordance with Rules, and only way to communicate with Board because Board advised Management Company to Ignore all correspondence from me regarding this issue.

Noise Issues:

- This has been frustrating for us all. It is my opinion that Management Company wasted over 10,000 on unnecessary consultant fees, and never implemented most of the recommendations.
- Another co-op is suing Management Company for non-delivery of services etc. Trial Date Oct 2020.
- Management Company issued incorrect terms of

Join a Housing Co-op. What Could Go Wrong?

reference to BAP and had to be called back.
- BAP report and Outcome letter – no mention of Transformer in Management Company Report but clearly an issue in BAP report.
- Management Company had no electrician, and illegally gave master keys to an unknown electrician who entered my unit without authorization. Management Company claimed someone was home. I live alone.
- Recommendations by Mechanical Consultant from Management Company were ignored.
- Consultants were called in during the daytime when the noise does not happen and did not contact me to discuss the nature of the noise issue.

Definition of Conduct Detrimental to the Co-op

5.2 **Conduct detrimental to the Co-op**

Conduct detrimental to the Co-op can include, but is not limited to, such things as:

[a] failure to comply, or failure to ensure compliance by any resident or person visiting the member, with any term or provision of:

[1] these Rules or the Occupancy Agreement; or

[2] any Policy which may be in effect;

[b] causing, permitting, or threatening wilful damage to the property or physical premises of the Co-op or the Unit;

Items listed in the 13 allegations do not meet the definition of "conduct detrimental to the Co-op.

77

I'm on heavy duty sleeping pills with a brown noise generator turned to try to on so I can sleep
- My letters all start with a call to help.

[c]	causing, permitting, or threatening violence directed against persons on the Co-op's property;
[d]	unauthorized detention of property of the Co-op;
[e]	causing, permitting, or threatening injury or harm to the reputation of the Co-op; or
[f]	repeated late payment of Housing Charges.

Despite a request to do so, no listing of what statements are offensive have been provided,

No explanation been offered as to how my behavior is detrimental to the co-op

The 13 claims are a twisting of facts, innuendo and exaggerations.

Particulars of the of the conduct complained of are:

1. On or about March 15, 2019, you became aggressive and yelled at director Raoul when speaking with him regarding your noise complaints. This discussion occurred outside of a board meeting. You were notified previously by management that Board members are unable to discuss Co-op matters outside of Board meetings. Please see attached email from Raoul dated March 15, 2019 which describes this incident;

- No complaint has been communicated to me from Raoul. This was from over 1 year ago.

Join a Housing Co-op. What Could Go Wrong?

- This is unequal treatment of members – from The Jan 2020 Board Meeting Minutes:

  "7.2.1. The Board prefers that complainants address their concerns directly with the person(s) whom they have an issue with, either in written format or face-to-face in person

  7.2.2. The Board suggests both parties sit down, discuss issue and make a compromise on situation "

- I was recovering from hernia surgery and had not been able to sleep for weeks while trying to recover from surgery. I could not sleep in my unit due to the noise that the Board determined to be 'credible' as stated in the minutes.

- I was seeking assistance but Raoul's response was confrontational, and his responses were unhelpful contributing to greater stress. He kept trying to trip me up, focusing on single words as I explained to him that I was suffering from sleep deprivation. He kept repeating false statements made by Gillian and was behaving as though he was trying to cross-examine me. Raoul walked away, and I broke down in tears, then sought mental health treatment.

- I was never notified by management that Board members were not to discuss with me and this would be in violation of Principles of Natural Justice and unequal treatment of members. No other member is under this new rule. No notice was ever sent to me.

- The direction to not talk to me was not voted upon until the Board meeting of Jan 2020.
- After that incident I wrote an apology note to Raoul. The issue was never brought up again until now.
- In the spring of 2019 Raoul started an extremely loud gas powered lawn trimmer outside my unit at 9:03 am on a Sunday morning of a long weekend. He ran the lawn trimmer wearing earplugs only near my unit and then stopped after about 10 minutes. I did not yell at him, but calmly said "Raoul, this may be legal but it's not helpful." I assumed that this was not a harassment issue but that Raoul had not thought through his actions.
- This spring, when politely asking Raoul to discuss this noise issue, Raoul yelled at me "NO!"
- There is no basis for this being grounds for termination.

2. You have engaged in a pattern of aggressive and harassing behavior towards the authorized agents of the Co-op's, Management Company. Despite the Co-op's and Management Company's efforts to respond in a timely and efficient manner to your noise complaints, you continue to send many emails regarding the same. This results in overusing the management time allotted by Management Company to the Co-op as a whole and inhibits Management Company's ability to attend other management matters. In addition, you continue to allege mismanagement, malfeasance and delay of

Join a Housing Co-op. What Could Go Wrong?

investigations related to sourcing the noise issue despite the Co- op arranging for repeated investigations by several tradespeople, electricians and engineers. You continue to wrongfully accuse Management Company through posting negative comments onto social media websites such as Yelp and Facebook. Among other things, you have continuously, and wrongly, accused Management Company of various items of malfeasance and even mental health status. Please see attached letter from the Co-op dated March 26, 2019;

- Management Company is a third party and the Board has no authority in my relationship with Management Company. It is not "conduct detrimental to the Co-op"

- If the co-op were to fix this noise issue none of these issues would have happened.

- I dispute the language that it was aggressive and harassing. I was always polite.

- I have not received any notice from Management Company itself regarding my actions.

- Regarding Facebook, Since Management Company would not respond to my emails to resolve the noise issue, I posted a request to Management Company to fix the noise issue, as do many customers of other organizations.

- Management Company responded on Facebook revealing personal information and repeating falsehoods. I felt this was going nowhere so I deleted all messages myself.

- There are no posts on social media. I did not post on yelp. I can provide concrete examples of Management Company's mistakes if you wish to hear them.

- No copies of these posts have been provided.

- The co-op has no authority over third parties. There is no rule about this in the Occupancy Agreement, Rules or Policy

- Management Company and the co-op has not tried to resolve this in an efficient and timely manner. See timeline provided to CRT.

- The behavior has been reasonable in accordance with the issues I am experiencing, and Management Company was issued a Cease and Desist notice for their own derogatory comments and repeating falsehoods about me.

- Regarding a letter I wrote to the Board and the reply accusing me of derogatory comments, I wrote to Management Company asking what the derogatory comments were and did not receive any response.

- Based on legal advice, wrote Cease and Desist letters to Management Company, The Board, Gillian and David and Libby to get them to stop making these false accusations and for making derogatory comments about me, and providing false information to other parties.

- Regarded allotted time, that is not grounds for termination. As explained to Raoul, and as he requested, I provide a copy of an email from Management Company stating they had no electrician, and that they were spending a huge amount of their time phoning around trying to find an electrician.

> "XXXX is our designated-on call electrician, when he was hospitalized that left us with no on call electrician on hand, which is why we had to start calling around to locate an electrical firm who was even willing to come in after hours. "

- I came home one day to find an unidentified man in my unit. Remaining calm, I asked him to identify himself. He said he was an electrician contracted by Management Company to investigate an electrical issue in my unit. He told me he had been given master keys to the whole building. He wanted to give the master keys to me for return to Management Company but I refused. I complained to Management Company about this and Raoul stated that Management Company said that someone was home to let him in. I live alone.

- Management Company issued incorrect terms of reference to Acoustics Engineers and they had to return to do the proper work. Furthermore, Management Company made a serious error in the report they sent to the Board, ignoring the issue of the Distribution Box, which was referred to as the Transformer. Acoustic Engineers acknowledge this error.

3. Despite being advised by the Co-op as set out in the letter dated March 26, 2019 regarding the Co-op's position on Management Company, you continued to

disparage Management Company and allege malfeasance by Management Company. Please see attached correspondence dated April 23, 2019 and March 25, 2020;

- Again, Management Company is a third party, has been issued a Cease and Desist letter, is being sued by another co-op for similar issues.
- Management Company has not filed any complaint directly with me.
- The board has no jurisdiction in this matter.
- Writing to my MP and MLA for help is not "conduct detrimental to the co-op" nor has your letter shown how it is qualifies as such. It was a call for help, because the Board and Management Company would not listen

4. On January 15, 2020, you approached member Theresa in an aggressive manner. You further attempted to discuss matters that should be brought to the attention of a Board member only during a formal Board meeting. Please see enclosed the e-mail to Management Company from member Theresa dated January 15, 2020 reporting this incident;

- I dispute that I was aggressive. I was at all times polite and respectful.
- The following week we met at the elevator and we both exchanged pleasantries. I expressed to her that I was deliberately not bringing up co-op issues in our conversation. She thanked me and said

Join a Housing Co-op. What Could Go Wrong?

"That's great! We're back to being good neighbors!"

- There had been no notice given to me that I could not speak to Board members.

- This is a member to member issue and no complaint was received from Theresa until I received the Termination notice.

- Unequal treatment of members: From the Board meeting of Jan 2020

- Member to Member complaints – See Dispute policy.

5. On February 24, 2020, your CRT claim against the Co-op was settled and a formal consent order was issued (the "Order"). You have violated the Order by refusing to move to unit #224 despite the Co-op and members incurring costs and time in attempting to make the unit available and follow the Order. Furthermore, you have violated the Order by requesting the Co-op further inspect your unit for noise-related complaints. Enclosed is the letter from Management Company dated March 25, 2020 outlining your violation of the Order. We have also enclosed a copy of the CRT Order dated February 24, 2020 for your reference;

- As stated in my correspondence, the move was frustrated by Covid19.

- I also incurred expenses, time and effort in packing and preparing my unit for her.

- I painted two walls and with considerable effort

and expense repaired some defective laminate flooring boards requiring the removal of 75% of the flooring in my unit My letter to her state a request to discuss the matter.

- Public Health Emergency Orders take precedence over a negotiated move date.

- I requested that we discuss the matter, but instead the Co-op demanded that I repay $1350 and defaulted on other aspects of the Order.

- CRO states that "This order does not in any way affect the applicant's membership on the co-op"

- Now that Covid19 has settled and things are opening up, I emailed her requesting a new move date. She has not responded and is in default of the Tribunal Order.

- Next week the courts will open and I will be filing the CRO for enforcement.

- Submitting a work order is not the same as requesting a Move Out Inspection.

- Just after the CRO was issued, Management Company contacted me to arrange a Unit inspection of my unit for the move. I had to explain to the new employee that the CRO stated no unit inspections. Instead of filing a complaint for violating the CRO, I let it go, assuming it was a new employee not properly trained by her employer.

- Theresa is in default of the order and so is the Co-op.

Join a Housing Co-op. What Could Go Wrong?

- If you terminate my membership for defaulting, you must treat all members equally and terminate Theresa's membership.

6. On or about March 31, 2020, you wrote to Management Company and the Board of Directors alleging that member Theresa had mislead the Tribunal, lied and faced possible prosecution and imprisonment, all of which is untrue. Please find enclosed your letter dated March 31, 2020.

- This is for the courts to decide in a prosecution case. It is not grounds for termination. It is a member to member issue.

- The CRT provided me with links to proceed with prosecution.

Dear Mark OMeara

Thank you for contacting the Civil Resolution Tribunal.

Section 92 of the Civil Resolution Tribunal Act prohibits parties from providing false or misleading evidence or other information in a tribunal proceeding. If you believe a party has breached the section 92 of the Civil Resolution Tribunal Act, you are welcome to speak with the local police to ask them whether they want to pursue charges under the Offence Act. You can also go to the Provincial Court and lay an information under s. 11 of the Offence Act and that would begin the process of prosecuting it yourself. The Provincial Court Registry can give you more information.

The CRT doesn't have authority to investigate or prosecute offences; the provision in the Civil Resolution

Tribunal Act is there for the Crown or citizens to use in the event they have the will to pursue it.

- Theresa made claims which she had no right to make.
- In CRT negotiations, she stated the Electrical Panel is unrepairable, but Board minutes state it is repairable and $50,000 was authorized to repair it.

Board Minutes from: Feb 19 2019

4. Member invited to meeting

– AP maintenance chairperson – speaking to board on electrical inspection, yard work, catch basins, wireless cameras for B1.

Electrical inspection – did tour with XXX Electric and was shown issue and is concern about issues that were shown, board approved to have the quote approved to have work down just not on yearly basis but every 5 years the diagnosis can be done.

MOTION: *BIRT the board to approve for XXX Electric to run full electrical diagnostic on buildings and do necessary repair work to electrical system to eliminate noise it is causing and potential hazards. M/S/C*

Board Minutes from Sept 24 2019
Old Business 2.1 Ongoing noise complaint OMEARA, Mark

Discussed with engineer – complaints credible and backed up by report Management Company ordered.

Equipment old and low grade brand could be repaired. Equipment will have to be replaced in a few years – estimate

Join a Housing Co-op. What Could Go Wrong?

of the cost to replace and upgrade equipment in the $50,000 + range.

The BOD agreed that the member should call Management Company emergency line when the noise occurs who will contact the electrical engineer to do a site visit

- Prosecution is still an option, however I would prefer to resolve this matter amicably.

7. You have written to third parties seeking to injure the reputation of the Coop. Please see attach email from you to various government persons, institutions and regulatory authorities date March 31, 2020;

The intent of these letters was to seek help for a serious situation that the Co-op refuses to resolve. Doctors notes were provided attesting to the severe effect on my health.

- The negative reputation of the co-op precedes any of my correspondence as illustrated in comments made to me in a call with the Ministry of Urban Affairs and Housing. I was told the Ministry is well aware of this co-op.

- Numerous requests for mediation have gone unanswered.

- Writing to my MP or MLA to ask for help is not grounds for termination. It was a call for help, because the Board, and Management Company would not help me.

- The need to write these letters stems from the Co-op's dysfunctional behavior.

8. You have, on at least two occasions since April 1, 2020, contacted and had police attend at Theresa's suite because of her ceiling fan thereby causing Theresa to feel threatened and harassed;

- City of Burnaby Noise Bylaw Enforcement Officer advised me that it was a police issue and to call the Police.

- First occasion: Police (Constable XXX) asked for contact member for a Board member. They talked to Theresa and got nowhere and referred me to Victim Services to try to help me.

- Maintenance Volunteer came to investigate the noise issue and knocked on Theresa's door and requested that she turn off her ceiling fan to eliminate it as the cause of the noise that Maintenance Volunteer confirmed to be present. Theresa refused to do so.

- The member is in violation of the good neighbor policy.

- Although unfortunate to have to resort to calling the police a second time, again it was under the advice of the City of Burnaby Noise Bylaw Enforcement officer/ It is my right to do so under these circumstances.

- I called the Police about the noise issue, not

specifically about Theresa.

- The officer looked up the previous file number and on that basis, decided to contact Theresa on his own initiative. I did not suggest he contact Theresa. His actions were based on his own decision while trying to seek out a Board member.

- The officer was frustrated because, again, Theresa refused to co-operate. He advised me that Theresa had requested a "do not contact" order but he felt it was unnecessary and would not be helpful and did not issue any such order. Theresa that an order was issued to me is false and she is misleading the Board.

- Calling the Police for a noise bylaw violation is not harassment, nor is it grounds for termination.

- Theresa's refusal to co-operate under the "Good Neighbor" Policy resulted in her own misfortune.

9. On or about April 29, 2020, you wrote to both the Board and to Theresa complaining again about the ceiling fan in Theresa's unit and threatening Theresa with membership termination proceedings. Please find attached your letters dated April 29, 2020 with attachments;

- See number 8

- Theresa is in violation of the Good Neighbor

Policy and the Board did not take any action on my Grievances. This constitutes unequal treatment of members.

- Theresa is not describing incidents correctly. Regarding her claim that I was taping up a notice in the elevator and ranting, the facts are that: the elevator was broken and not working so as a good Neighbor I put up notices. She came out of her unit and I explained that the elevator was broken and that I had called the Management Company Emergency Line to report it, but Management Company did not answer the Emergency Line. I did not rant, there are no other witnesses other than Theresa.

- Theresa is clearly showing a pattern of using inflaming and false language to describe polite and amicable situations.

- Equal treatment of members means that the Board must investigate my complaints and follow the Policy Manual and rules just as it has with Theresa's complaints.

- The Board is in violation of Rule 6.03 – Uniform Application.

Join a Housing Co-op. What Could Go Wrong?

6.03 <u>Uniform application</u>

Unless otherwise specifically provided therein, all Rules, this Occupancy Agreement and Policies shall apply to all members of the Co-op uniformly and without preference or discrimination.

10. On May 1, 2020, you visited Theresa's unit and demanded that Theresa turn off her ceiling fan. Theresa expressed that she was frightened as you remained outside her unit door, and Theresa did not leave her unit that morning for fear of running into you again. Theresa considered this incident to be an instance of harassment. Please see enclosed the email from Theresa to the Board dated May 1, 2020 which describes this incident;

- Knocking on her door was advise of the RCMP non-emergency dispatch. I politely requested, not demanded.

- I politely asked her as "a good Neighbor" saying "would you please just help?"

- Theresa has a consistent approach of using strong language that inflames the description.

- She did not express any fright, and I did not remain at her door as she claims.

- Theresa's email contains false allegations that I am targeting women and further action against

93

Theresa may be initiated for slander/libel.

- I empathize that her anxiety is real, but I am not the cause of it.

11. On May 1, May 2 and May 3, 2020 you called the emergency line of Management Company Management after hours for non-emergency purposes to report additional noise complaints. Please see enclosed the summary report dated May 7, 2020 of after hours phone calls from Management Company Management which describes these incidents;

- My mediation agreement defines this situation as an emergency

- I was following instructions from the Board to do this. (See Board minutes)

- This call was in accordance with my Mediation agreement, defining an emergency as that affects a members health. I was unable to sleep for a number of nights and was in bad shape, and have numerous doctors notes. This issue qualifies as an emergency.

- The policy written by Management Company was never voted on by membership and therefore is not official policy.

12. On May 4, 2020, you wrote a letter to the Board regarding your noise complaints and challenged the Co-op's and Management Company's investigations and actions following the reports from the Acoustic

Engineer. You also posted the letter to the unit doors of all Board members against the Co-op's policy and after being notified by Management Company to not do so. Please see enclosed your letter to the Board dated May 4, 2020. Please also see enclosed emails to Management Company from Board members XXX and YYYY stating that the same was posted to their doors.

- It is not a crime nor grounds for termination to write a letter to the Board. The correspondence was delivered in accordance with the Rules and Regulations and Occupancy Agreement.

- A letter given to Management Company to give to Board members was withheld from the Board.

- Notices were posted on ALL board members doors in accordance with Rule and Regulations and Occupancy Agreement

- Management Company has no authority to dictate new policy to members.

- I have not received any complaint from Vivian.

- These letters were delivered in accordance with the rules. The rule was clearly stated on the letter.

13. On May 4, 2020, the Board received a complaint regarding your behavior from Vivian Please see enclosed emails from Vivian dated May 4, 2020 which describes this incident.

- This is a member to member issue and should be

dealt with according to the official Policy Manual.

- Again, this is unequal treatment of me: The minutes of Jan 2020 state the Board prefers members resolve issues among themselves.

- Until I received the notification regarding termination, I was never informed of this complaint.

- Vivian seems unaware that Board addresses were provided to me by Management Company management as required by law.

- Regarding the discussion of the new member in 117, I have had three conversations with her.

    1) I advised her that her smoke detector had gone off at 6:30 and that she should get it checked.

    2) I asked her how she was doing and she said she was power-washing her patio We had a friendly discussion and I mentioned she should get a lock for her patio door as we have had break-ins and items being stolen from patios.

    3) I helped the former tenant's family with the disposal of his wheelchair and help my neighbor determine the correct locker. Management Company had given the wrong locker number to her so I advised her of the correct locker number.

    4) The member in 117 has not filed a complaint, we only have an email that Thresa wrote and is hearsay.

Join a Housing Co-op. What Could Go Wrong?

That covers all the allegations.

Things I do as a member:

- 5 printers left at the garbage bin – took them to recycling
- Fire extinguisher – found a recycling depot and paid the fee.
- Plants outside – repotted them and brought them back to life
- Patio stones – moved them to the side of the building.
- Derelict XXXX sign – cleaned, restored and painted to make the place look nice
- Planters at front of building- dead plants removed and purchased new plants
- Algae infection at front of building and entrance – cleaned it all up on my own initiative
- Reporting that Tool room was left unlocked by Management Company
- Reporting that Electrical room left unlocked by Fire-pro.
- Reporting flooding of locker room.
- When ambulances or Fire dept or police arrive at building I respect privacy of member but let them into building.
- Someone forgot to send out Rent increase update so I politely reminded them.
- Taking out recycling bin from lobby when volunteer forgets to do it and putting it back.
- Intervened to protect a senior member being abused and threatened by a homeless person.

- Called 911 for him.
- Cleaning up around garbage bins and dealing with large item pickups left at our curb.
- After my neighbor passed away, helped family deal with Electric Chair, repairing it, and storing it for a month till they donate it, and helping find correct locker.
- Weeding of Building 2 front and organizing volunteers.
- When Ann-Marie's daughter fell on the balcony I checked to make sure she was ok.
- When there was a loud thump and screaming from above (Theresa's unit) I made sure they were both ok and excused myself when it became a family matter.
- Elderly confused lady wandering in snow in park I called 911 and stayed with her.
- Driving a member to hospital for emergency MRI when garage door wouldn't open.
- Helping a neighbor shred personal and financial documents to avoid identity theft from people going through recycling bins.

What does Termination accomplish?

- More pain, for me, for the Board, and for my friends in the co-op who lose a valuable member, and for the reputation of the co-op.
- It will be far more expensive than to just fix the noise issue.
- It will result in a general meeting with a special

Join a Housing Co-op. What Could Go Wrong?

  resolution in which everything discussed in this meeting will be presented to the membership.
- I have no reservations about sharing any of these accusations with the membership.
- It will be divisive and disturb other members and you will likely face a backlash from the membership.
- When I file the CRO in the court, if my unit is occupied by someone else, I will get Ann- Marie's unit as dictated by the court order and she will have to move to anther possibly smaller unit if one is available.
- It will result in significant legal costs to the co-op to go to the Supreme Court.
- Please rethink and listen to my version of events as they differ greatly from the other persons narrative.

In summary,

- All 13 issues have been discounted in this reply.
- Theresas allegations are exaggerations and leave out significant events to even further exaggerate her claims.
- Her stress due to Covid19 is not my fault.
- The noise issue still needs to be urgently resolved. What would you do in my shoes?
- I'm hoping that you will hear my side of the story, and given these details, you can understand that I had very limited options.
- If you go ahead with termination, we will end up with a Special Resolution at a General Meeting at which all of this will be presented to the Membership.

- I am a very open person. I have no reservations about sharing any of these issues including my reply with the membership.
- It will be divisive and disturb other members and you will likely face a backlash from the membership.
- There are no grounds for termination. It is a bad attempt at a solution, and mediation could resolve this.
- This is an extremely frustrating situation for all of us.
- All my letters were a call for help.
- You have not shown how my letters are "conduct detrimental to the Co-op"
- I am defending my Human Right to housing. This is my home and I am defending that right.

I end the presentation with the following statement:

"The most courageous people to me are those who are willing to look at themselves and admit they have a mindset that is part of the problem and knowing it can be changed for the better."

The mindset here is not solving the problem.

Again, I request mediation. I am appealing to your sense of justice, and I trust that you will hear this with honor, respect, and due diligence, and that a peaceful resolution can occur.

Join a Housing Co-op. What Could Go Wrong?

Terminated! I Appeal

At the meeting my lawyer failed to do anything. He didn't present any cases or warn the co-op about the human rights violations I was experiencing. He tried to enforce recording the meeting, but the co-op lawyer insisted that would not happen. He asked one Board member if he would consider what I presented. Later he said he was trying to establish bias. My lawyer just simply said "We will wait for your decision." He got up and left.

I received notice one day later that my membership was being terminated. My presentation and effort to resolve things had failed. The lawyer billed me for over $1700 even though we had agreed on $1500. He extra billed for research on "principles of social justice" I paid the $1500 and protested the extra charge as this should be knowledge the lawyer should already possess. The letter from the co-op lawyer stated that anything in my presentation could be used against me. My lawyer had failed in the most basic of principles to tell me to write "without prejudice" on my presentation.

I filed a notice to appeal my termination. This would involve calling a general meeting of the co-op, which was unlikely due to the ongoing Covid restrictions and need for social distancing and wearing a mask. I thought I had some breathing room.

A few weeks later the courts re-opened. I filed the CRT order in both provincial and Supreme courts. This now made the CRT order enforceable. Prior to filing it, the order was not enforceable.

Termination Meeting Announced!

A month later I got a notice that the termination meeting was going forward. The co-op sent out a lengthy document outlining all the accusations against me and the false narrative they had used for my Board termination. Despite my refuting all the claims they made they still proceeded with all the false allegations.

The co-op has gone to considerable effort to set up software for a hybrid meeting. The meeting would be both in-person and online. The meeting was scheduled for Sept 20th, 2020. I need legal assistance but can't afford it.

A package similar to my original termination notice is sent to all 100 plus members of the co-op. Despite my presentation at the Board meeting, the package contains all the allegations, less the allegations of the President Raoul. There are now 11 allegations. Writing the letter to my MLA and other officials is considered "Conduct Detrimental to the Co-op. Following the advice of the Board to call the emergency number is grounds for termination. They falsely claim I made derogatory comments on Facebook about the Management Company. They claim that by leaving two letters in a period of two months delivered to the Board members' residences is harassment even though the rules state this is a legitimate form of communication. One Board member complains that she feels unsafe because I left the notice on her door and is wondering how I got her address. Clearly, she has not had Board training, nor is she aware the addresses of the Board were provided by the Co-op's Management Company

I feel thoroughly embarrassed and ashamed by this action of the Board. Some Neighbors come up to me and state that they will support me because they feel I am being railroaded out of the co-op. Other members say they side with me but do not want to get involved because the Co-op mafia will give them trouble. Other members with whom I had a good relationship start avoiding me and acting strangely towards me.

An Offer to Resolve

I reach out to my MLA for assistance. I'm crying on the phone when her office calls back and says they have someone who can assist me. I'm exhausted both mentally and physically.

Join a Housing Co-op. What Could Go Wrong?

The advocate speaks with me, and I send him my collection of documentation. He writes the following letter on my behalf:

To: [CO-OP], [CO-OP LAWYER]

Re: Mark O'Meara

I act on behalf of Mark O'Meara. I will shortly be forwarding an authorization for representation and consent for disclosure signed by Mr. O'Meara.

I understand that the membership of [XXXX] Housing Cooperative (the Co-op) will be voting on 2020 September 17 on whether to terminate Mr. O'Meara's membership within the Co-op. I believe there is still opportunity to resolve this issue in the best interests of both parties. No doubt it has come to the point where the Board wants closure. I do not think that this vote provides closure. Rather, I suspect that neither the Board nor Mr. O'Meara will be happy with either outcome. Set out below is our proposal to resolve the issue, and we will accept any reasonable additions:

We propose the following:
- That Co-op, in whatever fashion complies with the rules, cancel the vote to terminate membership
- That both parties waive their rights to pursue these matters in the Human Rights Tribunal (BCHRT), the Civil Resolution Tribunal (CRT) and the BC Supreme Court.
- That [THE CO-OP] offer the first available 1-bedroom suite to Mr. O'Meara. Mr. O'Meara prefers a similar-sized unit in the same building, so while this type of suite might not come up as first offer, Mr. O'Meara requests an opportunity to apply for such a suite in the future, and the Co-op may wish to give Mr. O'Meara preference over an external candidate

- That Mr. O'Meara will only speak to the Board in writing
- Please consider the potential litigation that may follow this vote:

BC Civil Resolution Tribunal – Mr. O'Meara has filed to enforce the CRT's previous order. The co-op will face expense in responding to this. Further, Mr. O'Meara has a potential claim for a breach of quiet enjoyment. The payment made as part of the 2020-02-24 agreement may have included a quiet enjoyment settlement but Mr. O'Meara may choose to file a claim for the subsequent period.

BC Supreme Court – Mr. O'Meara has the right of appeal following this vote. Even if Mr. O'Meara were unsuccessful in such a claim, the Co-op will need to pay for further legal fees to respond. Further, there is no guarantee that the Co-op would be the successful party in such a claim. In the event an amicable settlement can't be reached between Neighbors, I expect that Mr. O'Meara would obtain counsel and pursue every legal remedy available to him at Court. I'm sure your own counsel would agree that litigation at Court is risky, time consuming, and expensive.

BC Human Rights Tribunal – Mr. O'Meara may bring a human rights complaint against the Co-op. In Redmond v. Hunter Hill Housing Co-op ((No. 2), 2013 BCHRT 276 (CanLII)) the BCHRT upheld a claim of discrimination against a housing co-op when it failed to investigate what was required to accommodate a woman and her children who were experiencing asthma due to mould allergies in their apartment unit.

Instead of accepting that the woman had a legitimate

problem, the housing co-op was adversarial, did not respond to the member's concerns, and communicated only with threatening letters from lawyers. In the same case, the member was successful in her claim before the BCHRT after merely indicating insomnia. The BCHRT ruled that the housing co-op had a duty to inquire about the member's underlying health in order to determine their duty to accommodate.

Mr. O'Meara is prepared to work to resolve issues between him and the Co-op amicably, and we hope the Co-op will consider this as well.

We question whether the funds and time that will be expended to attempt to terminate Mr. O'Meara's membership, and the resulting acrimony between Neighbors is in the best interests of the Co-op members. The Board serves the membership: Do members wish to put their housing costs into legal battles?

If the vote proceeds, I will be attending to support Mr. O'Meara and make submissions as his representative. I encourage you to take action to ensure the vote does not escalate the issue.

Please let us know as soon as possible if you will consider our proposal and whether the vote will proceed so that we can plan accordingly.

With thanks,

[COMMUNITY ADVOCATE]

The Co-op does not respond to the letter. In my talks with the Advocate, I learn he is not a lawyer but someone who works on the behalf of poor people with housing issues.

CRT Complaints Stalled

I'm trying to proceed with the Civil Resolution Tribunal, but the Co-op has filed a motion to dismiss. I am given only a few days to respond. I request an extension, stating that I'm dealing with depression and suicidal thoughts and exhaustion from not being able to sleep in my unit. The CRT forwards this confidential reply to the co-op. I tell the CRT agent that this was a violation of my privacy. My advocate sends them a tersely worded letter that they need to follow privacy laws. The co-op responds, denying the request but it is granted anyways by the CRT, but then tells me the complaint is being put on hold by the Tribunal pending the outcome of the termination meeting. The co-op is claiming that if my membership is terminated, I have no right to pursue the complaint. They also make a false claim that I assaulted co-op members.

My blood pressure is dangerously high. I'm suffering from bouts of crying. I can't sleep because of the noise. I'm having nightmares of being homeless and being hopeless and with severe anxiety. My family doctor refers me for counselling with the local mental health unit. I get a call from a counsellor and start counselling.

I Find a New Place – It's Time To Leave

The day of my termination meeting arrives. The meeting is happening tonight at 7pm. In the afternoon I post on Facebook asking where people look for apartments other than Craigslist. A few people provide suggestions. One suggestion is Padmapper.com. I go on that site and spot a very nice semi-basement in the same area for $1400. It's a two bedroom in a

Join a Housing Co-op. What Could Go Wrong?

brand-new house. I message the agent, and he responds quickly. He says they are showing it at 5pm and I can view it then. I'm there at 5 pm. It's a lot smaller than what I have but it would do. As I'm talking to the agent the landlord comes in. She's Chinese so I speak to her in Chinese which impresses her. I've already filled out the application with employment and references. As I'm signing the application, the agent gets a call and in a few moments he tells me the place is mine.

Going to the meeting, I know that I can move out into a quiet place and end this horror story.

The Termination Meeting

The meeting time comes, and I attend online. There are approximately 30 people present, including the Board of seven members - out of over one hundred co-op members. Both David and Libby are attending – David attends in person and Libby attends online. I can also see their daughter is online.

There are about 30 members present out of more than one hundred and thirty co-op members and associate members including the seven board members who will clearly vote in favor of my termination. The meeting has the necessary quorum of fifteen percent of members.

My advocate explains that the noise is a problem for me, that the harassment has left me traumatized and suicidal. He also explains that all of this seems to be the work of one person. He then introduces a very strange strategy that shocks me. He says that "the letter Mark wrote to his MLA, well when we get these, we just delete them, so no detrimental comments occurred." WTF? I feel floored. He just reduced my well written call for help to suggest that I'm a crazy person and they just deleted the letter.

President Raoul incorrectly quotes the Acoustic Engineer report stating that these were my words, and that I stated that all ambient noise ended when equipment was turned off. He doesn't continue reading the next part of the report confirming the low frequency noise from the transformer and electrical equipment and multiple overtones. He claims the co-op spent over twenty thousand dollars trying to solve this issue. He lists all the noises I've ever complained about. I go to speak up, but my advocate speaks over me and filibusters to prevent me from speaking. A few people get up to speak who have never met me or have limited knowledge. One lady speaks spiritedly rousing up a round of applause against me. She's never had a conversation with me. I'm clearly being scapegoated for the expenses and mistakes of the management company and the Board.

The advocate presents that my case is similar to another human rights case a co-op with the same Management company and that this will be very expensive to the co-op. The lawyer responds that the case referred to was with completely different ownership of the management company and that the co-op's insurance would cover any costs. Both of these claims turn out later to be complete lies. The management company's principle owner is still the same.

There are some people at the meeting who are good friends and support me. The voting takes place with both paper ballots and online ballots. For some reason I never receive my ballot. There are a total of 11 motions to terminate my membership. This is a method used to game the termination. If any one of the motions pass, then my membership will be terminated.

I never get a chance to speak and present my side of the story. My advocate has advised against this. The voting takes place. The motions pass with about 70-75% in favor of termination my membership. Only one or two votes would have made a difference.

Join a Housing Co-op. What Could Go Wrong?

I find it ironic that the co-op hasn't voted on anything for years, but the only vote that comes from my push for actual democratic control as per co-operative principles is my termination.

I am evicted. Now they must decide when. David and Libby's daughter puts on a very kindhearted demeanor despite her normally calling me hideous, glaring at me, or trying to hit me with her shopping cart, or telling her kids "do not talk to that hideous man" She is suggesting that I be given two months to move out, which is actually just the law. I ensure that the wording is "before Nov 1" not "on November 1st. This would allow me to meet the terms of my termination by moving out immediately.

I feel a huge loss. About an hour after the meeting, I decide to go for a walk. As I walk out of the meeting Theresa comes into the building. She looks very somber. My intuition tells me that the co-op lawyer has warned her and the board that their behavior was completely inappropriate and leaves the co-op wide open for a lawsuit and human rights complaint.

Should I Appeal to the Supreme Court?

In a co-op termination the member has thirty days to file a notice to appeal to the Supreme Court. I speak to a pro-bono lawyer who tells men that I could easily lose on a legal technicality. If I lose I will be held responsible for both my legal fees and the co-op's legal fees which could likely be around thirty five thousand dollars. I can't risk losing that money as it would bankrupt me. I don't have the financial resources to appeal. Furthermore, appealing would mean I would be staying in my noisy current unit and would be unable to sleep.

The Move-Out Inspection

I arrange to immediately move to the new apartment. I start selling some of my furniture. I hire movers and start packing. The new place does not have a dining area, and the combined kitchen and living room is tiny compared to my co-op unit. I move everything but quickly discover my couch doesn't fit in the living room. I have to get a smaller bed as my current bed won't fit in my small bedroom.

Getting Ready for the Move-out Inspection

I have to get ready for a move-out inspection at the co-op. I know that if my unit is not in perfect shape the co-op will give me an extravagant bill for repairs.

Over the next two weeks I repair any nail marks in the walls, repair any baseboards that had damage, and paint the whole apartment to be ready for an inspection. The Management Company inspector comes in and she starts to ask about the flooring. I state that it was approved by the Co-op, and I still have the documents. She then complains that I've left curtain rods on the dining room window. I left the security bars for the bedroom window and show her the defect in the window design allowing for an easy break in. She agrees those should stay but that I need to remove the curtain rods. I agree to do that the next day.

The next day I remove the curtain rods and spackle the holes and paint the affected area. She returns for another inspection, and I hand in all the keys. She tells me how she arranged for the remodeling of the unit across from me. I tell her about the horror stories with the Co-op and her management company. She says this is good to know because she is considering job options. I remind her that her employer is not a licensed property management company. She expresses surprise and apologies for what I've been through. I make sure that I get a signed statement that all issues with the unit have been remedied and resolved and that all keys have been returned.

I leave the apartment for the last time. While happy that I've found a new home, I feel grief over losing a large apartment at low

Join a Housing Co-op. What Could Go Wrong?

rent, but also for the friends I had there. Although there was trouble from a small core of people referred to as the mafia, at least 6 people of the 30 that showed up supported me. In the past few days many people dropped by or spoke to me in the hallway or garage to say goodbye and that it was the co-op's loss to have kicked me out. At anytime I could walk out of my unit and say hello to a friendly neighbor. I will miss that.

As I leave for the last time, the neighbor across the hall is going out. I take the opportunity to talk to her. I say "I'm sorry if my talking to you was in any way inappropriate. I just wanted to welcome you to the co-op, that's all." She replied "Oh it's no problem, thank you though for being so considerate. The politics of this co-op are really strange. That lady upstairs from you tried to get me to file a complaint against you, but I said no." I replied, "Well she reported me to the police for talking to you… and she successfully got me evicted." She looked shocked and dismayed. I said goodbye and left. I didn't have the heart to tell her that she was being moved to a two bedroom directly below David and Libby's daughter, who vacuums at all hours of the night and that if she files a complaint she'll likely be harassed.

Elevator Noise Disappears

I bump into a former member at the grocery store. She mentions that something strange happened at the co-op in our building. When in the basement elevator lobby, that noise that the elevator would make has completely stopped.

Threats from the Management Company

I'm now in my new place trying to make everything fit. To protect myself from unauthorized withdrawals I put a stop order on any withdrawals from the co-op for rent. That was a good idea because the Co-op and Management Company try to withdraw housing charges even though I have moved out. Even though my

111

Mark Linden O'Meara

membership has been terminated and I've moved out having completed a satisfactory move-out inspection I receive a letter threatening me with termination if I don't pay outstanding housing charges and that my arrears will be reported to the Credit Bureau.

Encounter at the Grocery Store

A few weeks later I'm at the grocery store and I spot David outside at the exit.

From: Mark OMeara

Sent: Tuesday, October 13, 2020 7:55 AM

To: CO-OP, CO_OP LAWYER, Management Company PRESIDENT

Cc: ADVOCATE

Subject: Control Violent/Abusive Co-op Member/Employee, Stop Harassing Letters, and Demand for Payment

Attachments: Demand for Payment Oct 9 2020.pdf; IMG_0062.jpg

Importance: High

Please see attached, sent by registered mail.

Due to physical threats of violence and verbal abuse regarding my mental health from the co-op building manager David Allen on Friday Oct 9th requiring RCMP intervention File BU-XXXXXX please ensure my forwarding address remains confidential.

Also, I received the attached letter on Friday. Please stop these harassing letters. Please ensure that further withdrawal attempts are stopped and that you do not report

Join a Housing Co-op. What Could Go Wrong?

any transactions to the credit bureaus.

I encountered two co-op members at the grocery store on Friday. They told me that David Allen was telling people I had moved into XXX co-op and that he had seen me unloading stuff. This is completely false, and in violation of my mediation agreement of "no gossiping".

When I left the grocery store, David Allen was outside and I calmly and politely (using terminology from my non-violent communication course) suggested to him that I would appreciate it if he would stop spreading false information about me.

He exploded in anger, getting out of his wheel chair and came at me with fists raised and verbally abused me and threated to punch me out, challenging me to a fight. I walked away calling 911. I went around to the store entrance to ask for a pen to write down the Police Report number and he came around to the entrance and entered the store and cornered me at the customer service desk. He continued to threaten me saying "I'm going to take you apart" I escaped from the store with the help of store staff and security, but he started chasing me in his wheel chair yelling obscenities at me, verbally abusing me, calling me a f*kn mental case, and yelling that I was a sissy and a chicken,... and that he wanted to fight me. He kept yelling at me creating a scene and was trying to goad me into a fight,. I called 911 again, sought a safe place to talk to police. The RCMP advised me that they would speak to him once again and advise him that his behaviour was unacceptable.

This is at least the third time David has threatened me physically, verbally abused me. In one incident he threatened "to put me in the morgue". Each time I filed a grievance but nothing was done by the co-op. This is unacceptable. All members are to be treated equally and his threats continue unchecked. Please reign in this co-op member who claims to be the co-op Building Manager.

This verbal abuse, derogatory comments about my mental health, and threats of violence are not acceptable from anyone.

I am traumatized by this whole situation and require further counselling to deal with it. Stopping these harassing letters and unauthorized withdrawals would at least be the first step in minimizing the stress of this terrible situation. I expect the Board to proceed with a reprimand of Mr Allen and grievance against David for conduct detrimental to the Co-op and threatening behavior. As per the official policy manual (not the unapproved policy manual being distributed by Management Company -alteration requires Special Resolution), members have 6 months after leaving to file a grievance, which I am doing so with this letter.

Regards

Mark OMeara

The police never showed up, and later they said that they could not located him (even though I gave them his specific address) and they closed the file.

I decide to withdraw the CRT complaints so I could focus on my mental health. I'm a mess and still having nightmares and depression and anxiety. But even withdrawing the complaints takes a lot of work. I have to file documents, respond to the co-op's response etc. It's an extremely draining process to withdraw the complaints. The co-op is trying to get a ruling that the case has already been heard but the CRT declines.

Join a Housing Co-op. What Could Go Wrong?

Depression, Nightmares, High Blood Pressure

Although I've moved out, I'm severely depressed over what transpired. I'm having trouble sleeping. I'm waking up early in the morning. I think I have hearing damage from the ongoing low level noise at the co-op. I can't write. I have extremely high blood pressure. Every couple of days I have a nightmare where I'm still living in the co-op but suddenly realize I have to move and have no place to go and while people are friendly to me, I feel a deep sense of injustice. I'm having suicidal thoughts. I continue counselling.

For the next two years I have nightmares every two weeks. The dream is the same. I am living in the co-op getting along with neighbors then I realize that I still have the termination to deal with and although relationships are good, I have to leave in a few days and have nowhere to go. I am exhausted, and I still have very high blood pressure that is not responding to treatment. I've gained weight. I'm depressed.

I file a FOI with the co-op and their new lawyer (although with the same firm) responds that they will provide the information requested by a certain date. On that date the lawyer says they will provide nothing. The Privacy Office orders them to provide it.

Collecting Monies Owed

Based on the original CRT order, the co-op owed me $2700. I began the process of recovering that money through the court system. There were numerous steps – sending a demand letter, a waiting period, serving the co-op, another waiting period. Finally, I had a court garnishment order. I had kept the cheque I wrote to pay back the funds from the CRT order. Stamped on the back of the cheque was the bank. Account number and branch of the co-op's bank account. I presented the garnishment order to the bank and got my funds two weeks later.

Mark Linden O'Meara

A Government Roundtable Discussion on Reform

Having considerable knowledge of co-op legislation and co-op rules I write a report to the government on what needs to be changed in the laws and regulations. I am invited to attend a Roundtable discussion with senior co-op housing stakeholders. I will present my report. Other stakeholders echo the problems with the rules and regulations especially the advice to "talk to your board" and the issue of "conduct detrimental to the co-op" for which there is no definition. One organization mentions that they are seeing a sharp increase in Co-ops using this mechanism to evict people. To date the government has done nothing about it.

Submission Regarding BC Housing and |Co-operative Housing in BC
By Mark O'Meara, M.Ed, M.B.A.

Executive Summary

- Changes to the act governing Housing Co-ops by the previous Liberal government provided for increased Board power and a lack of scrutiny and accountability.
- Housing Co-ops are forgotten in legislation and government responses to issues.
- A loophole in the Real Estate Services Act allows unlicensed property management companies to operate outside of the law and are unregulated.
- Fraud can occur at Non-profit housing because of a lack of auditing standards and separation of duties (such as contracting process, review and

Join a Housing Co-op. What Could Go Wrong?

approval of invoices, and approval of payment by the same person). Members do not have access to spending details, and current board members do not have access to previous financial details.

- There are few legal resources for bullied or unfairly terminated co-op members. A search of appeals of termination with the court system reveals only one or two cases in the past twenty years.
- The threat of termination of a co-op member for "conduct detrimental to the co-op" amounts to a gagging of co-op members and is in conflict with whistle-blowing legislation.
- Legislative changes are required to ensure transparency, fairness, and accountability.
- Investment in Co-ops by BC Housing and through the Community Land Trust has had problems regarding construction quality and maintenance issues and ROI.
- The current legislation does not address "in camera" meetings by Co-op Boards.

My Summary and Experience

I moved into XXX Co-op in 2007 and soon became aware of dynamics in the Co-op. A group of us became aware of irregularities and asked to see financials. We identified that the co-op was helping the family who managed all committees to commit WCB fraud by paying the wife of the employee We also uncovered nepotism, kickbacks, a lack of transparency and wasteful spending. This was presented to the Board. They did nothing.

The 5 members involved began to experience

continued harassment. One of the group members was elected to the Board but not allowed to attend meetings. He was falsely accused of breaking a camera. For refused to pay an inflated repair bill he was removed from the Board.

Another member of the group was nominated but refused as a candidate after he refused to pay a highly inflated invoice for fixing a blocked toilet.

One disabled member was continually harassed and a number of attempts were made to terminate his membership. On the final termination attempt he died from a heart attack. The Board member who was central to this harassment gave the unit to her brother, who failed to pay his share purchase and failed to pay any housing charges for almost a year. After the new Board demanded payment, he was found dead in his unit. He committed suicide.

Another disabled member's subsidy was calculated incorrectly and while in the hospital to have his leg amputated, the board changed the locks on his unit, packed up his belongings and put them in storage. When he came out of the hospital he was homeless.

In 2022 a new treasurer had concerns about spending irregularities and asked for reports from the management company. He was accused of harassing office staff and removed from the Board.

I was a member of the original finance committee. From then on, I was harassed, verbally abused, threatened physically, received death threats and harassed with noise. RCMP were called numerous times and grievances filed but the Board did nothing. My unit experienced noise from malfunctioning equipment in the elevator, electrical, and boiler rooms directly below my unit.

Due to the noise I was sleeping in my car, in a tent on my patio, and I spent over $6000 on alternate sleeping

Join a Housing Co-op. What Could Go Wrong?

accommodations. RCMP were called numerous times. I was referred to Victim Services. I ended up at the ER numerous times for sleep deprivation and dangerously high blood pressure. The Board refused requests for mediation and ignored a previously negotiated mediation agreement.

A CRT agreement was reached but thwarted when COVID hit. When COVID subsided the Board refused to honor the CRT Court Order. My membership was then illegally terminated for writing to my MLA and MP for help, as this was considered by the Board to be 'conduct detrimental to the co-op.' because I harmed the reputation of the co-op by writing to my MP and MLA. I suffered PTSD and required two years of counselling to deal with the abuse I encountered and my loss of housing.

My knowledge of Co-op legislation and regulations, Civil Resolution Tribunal (CRT) procedures, and attempts to defend myself have given me valuable insight into the needed changes. I present these recommendations for your consideration.

Co-ops Are Forgotten

Unlicensed Property Management Companies Operating Due to Loophole

The Real Estate Services Act defines Real Estate Services as

- Sale transactions for property
- Strata management
- Rental properties where a lease is in place

Because Co-ops use the term "Occupancy Agreement" in place of lease, and the term "housing charges" instead of rent, the BC Financial Services Authority has determined that it has no jurisdiction over unlicensed property management companies providing property management services such as maintenance, budgeting, accounting, handling correspondence, emergency services etc., to Co-ops.

Eviction Protection During Covid.

Protections were put in place to protect renters. Co-ops were forgotten in that legislation. I was advised that a spike in terminations i.e. evictions from Co-ops occurred during Covid.

Rental Increase Protection

Again, Co-ops were forgotten in this legislation to protect people from significant housing cost increases.

Access to Legal Representation

There are less than a handful of law firms in BC specializing in Co-op Law. If any of the lawyers were a past lawyer, present lawyer or plan to become a lawyer for the co-op, they will not represent the member, due to a conflict of interest.

CHFBC has identified that legal representation for members instead of Boards is lacking and something they need to work on.

Access to an appeal of one's termination is prohibitively expensive and only available through the Supreme Court. I was advised that the appeal could cost the member upwards of $35,000 if unsuccessful and only had 30 days to do so. The Co-op Board has full access to the resources of the Co-op to fund a legal battle against a wrongfully terminated member.

No Remedy for Members When Board Doesn't Follow Law.

No remedy for instances of a Board not following the

Join a Housing Co-op. What Could Go Wrong?

laws or the co-op rules. CRT legislations states that the CRT does not rule on issues that are covered In legislation. CRT Rulings have stated that the CRT will not involve itself with issues covered in legislation and regulations.

The following list of organizations do not get involved in Co-op disputes.

- CHF-BC
- CHF Canada
- Tenant Resource and Advisory Centre (TRAC)
- BC Housing
- RCMP
- TECH BC
- BC Ministry of Health (in cases of health hazards)
- AGENCY (CMHC)
- Municipal Governments
- Ministry of Housing
- Better Business Bureau
- Office of the Superintendent of Real Estate
- Civil Resolution Tribunal (does not deal with Terminations nor will issue orders reflecting issues already covered in legislation)
- Victim Services of BC

Many of these organizations refer people to CHF-BC or CHF Canada, but all these organizations do is tell you to talk to your Board.

Legislation Changes That Harmed Co-Ops

In 2014, the Societies Act and subsequently, Occupancy Agreements were amended with the following major changes that impacted transparency and left the door open to fraud.

121

Board members and employees/contractors of the co-op could live in the same unit. Under the previous legislation and rules, this was not allowed. Also, the rule that two family members could not be on the board was removed. These rules were in place to provide a separation of duties as per standard accounting controls and to avoid family power dynamics.

Many organizations still have a rule in place where two family members can not be on a board.

Quorum reduced from 20% to 15%.

This reduction meant that in some smaller co-ops, the Board alone constituted quorum. The better idea would be to increase quorum to 30% to encourage participation and attendance at meetings. Quorum is 15% therefor in smaller co-ops, the Board is quorum for a termination. Even in a co-op with 100 members, the Board plus 8 members = quorum, and with a vote of 66% of those in attendance, only 10 people in the co-op of 100 are needed to terminate a membership at a meeting. The definition of quorum in the legislation is weak, as it does not specify whether voting associate members are to be included in the quorum calculations.

Reduction of number of meetings:

The minimum number of required general meetings was reduced. This reduced the opportunity for members to raise concerns or to participate in Co-op management discussions and decisions, or to raise concerns of accountability. Members can requisition a meeting by gathering signatures of 20% of members, but trying to do so in the current climate often leads to accusation of harassment by a Board for knocking on peoples' doors. Effectively, members have no method of requesting a meeting.

Join a Housing Co-op. What Could Go Wrong?

Transparency Issues

Under the current legislation

- There is no provision for members to see Board minutes.
- There is no requirement of the Board to convene a finance committee.
- There is no provision for members to examine the books or to request detailed financial transactions.
- There is no way to force a board to follow its rules.
- There is no provision in the legislation to deal with "in camera" Board minutes as there is in the Strata Regulations. In Co-ops, "in camera" meetings allow the board to discuss and decide issues without any record of the topic of the discussion or the outcome. This goes against the Co-op principles of transparency.
- While statements are audited for verifying numbers, no forensic audit occurs, allowing for fraud to easily occur.

Terminations and Timing of Meetings

If a Board decides to terminate a member, the member has only 7 days notice to attend a meeting of the Board. If given the notice on a Friday, as some co-ops do, the member only has 5 business days to find a lawyer and research and develop a response – 4 days if it is delivered on the Friday before a long weekend Renters get a minimum of 10 to 30 days notice.

If a Special meeting is called, the member only has 14 days to find a lawyer, research case law, and develop a legal strategy and response. This timeframe is inadequate.

This is completely unfair to the member. These timelines should be increased to at least 30 days notice and appeals to the Supreme Court should be a longer time frame as well.

The "Conduct Detrimental to the Co-op" Rule Harms Co-ops and Members

The Co-op legislation and Occupancy Agreement state that members can be terminated for "Conduct detrimental to the Co-op." There are various reasons given for termination under this clause is most troublesome and unfair: "a housing cooperative may terminate the membership of a member if the member has engaged in conduct detrimental to the housing cooperative".

This is essentially a gag order against members. No case law on the Canlii could be found regarding this section of the act or previous wordings of the act.

Speaking up to the media about an issue at the co-op could be considered such conduct.

In my case, writing to my MP and MLA asking for help was unfairly used as grounds for termination under this clause.

This rule serves as an anti-whistleblower tool and is in conflict with SLAPP legislation.

Under the "conduct detrimental" section, there is no provision in the act for the member to remedy the activity the Board has called into question BC HOUSING Involvement in Housing Co-ops

BC Housing provided a mortgage to help renovate the co-op I lived in. It was expected that a number of units be made available to low income people. A Board member initiated a refinancing of the BC Housing mortgage without the knowledge of the general membership. As a result, BC Housing was cut out of the picture and the co-op was no longer required to provide a number of units to low income members. Did BC Housing invest without a long term guarantee of a return?

BC Housing involves itself with Co-ops that are managed by unlicensed property management companies.

Join a Housing Co-op. What Could Go Wrong?

BC Housing, through the Community Land Trust, has provided funding for a number of co-ops that have had serious construction quality issues and have not operated at capacity due to high housing charges.

Even if BC Housing provides funding for a housing Co-operative, it refuses to get involved in Co-op disputes.

Some Co-ops Have Failed.

ABCDE Co-op closed. They were involved in a court battle with an unlicensed property management company who allegedly paid themselves tens of thousands of dollars using a House Charge authorization form to transfer the money. The money was returned after the RCMP became involved. The lawsuit alleged a number of other issues causing the Co-op to lose money due the alleged incompetence of the unlicensed property management company. This issue should be investigated more fully as to why various levels of government lost their investment.

Remedies Requested:

- Update the Societies Act and Real Estate Services Act to address the above concerns and loopholes.
- Empower the CRT deal with Co-op Terminations
- Provide legal assistance to members being terminated.
- Empower the CRT to issue orders if a Board is found to not be following its rules.
- Define and increase the function, role and responsibility of a Co-op's Auditor.
- Fix the loophole in the Real Estate Services Act to include Co-ops
- Legislate the minimum financial transparency requirements of co-ops, such as the threshold for members approving spending projects, the separation of duties, and the reconciliation of "housing charge"

income to expected income.

Outcome of the Meetings

Nothing was done. No report was issued. No action was taken to my knowledge. I contacted my MLA numerous times asking for the report but got no reply. MLA contacted the Ministry on my behalf and received a promise from them to contact me. Two months went by with no call, email or letter.

A Revealing Search of Court Records

Searching Civil Court records I find two cases initiated by the co-op against members. At least the co-op lawyer is advising them to follow proper procedure for evictions and reclaiming units.

In one case, an order of possession was obtained for against a member for his unit. He is found dead in his unit. He had been dead for a couple of weeks. It turns out this was Gillian's brother. Andy's unit became available after he survived numerous termination and eviction attempts by Gillian. The unit was given to her brother. Apparently, he never paid his share purchase upon moving in nor any of his rent. Somehow this went untracked for nine months.

Another Encounter at the Grocery Store

On a Saturday afternoon, at the grocery store, I encounter a co-op member who had been on the waiting list for a one bedroom. She had been living by herself in a two bedroom for years. My offer to the co-op and their earlier broken promise of offering me the next available one bedroom would have bumped her down the waitlist. She was at the next self=checkout. As I finished paying for my groceries and was leaving I said to her "I know that terminating my membership ensured your spot on the waitlist." I

Join a Housing Co-op. What Could Go Wrong?

continued to walk away but she followed me and started yelling at me. She yelled that she was going to call the police on me.

When I got home, I called the police non-emergency line and tried to report the encounter. The agent said that nothing reportable had happened so no report would be created and no action would be taken. I asked for his employee number and noted the time of my call and the outcome.

The next morning (a Sunday) my phone started ringing at 7am. The buzzing sound woke me up. It rang 5 times and noticing that a message had been left, I listened to the message. It was from the police. I called the officer back immediately.

It was about the incident the day before. He told me the co-op member was claiming that I was harassing her and she had called to complain. I explained to the officer rather explicitly that the co-op had been using the police to harass me. This discussion fired up all the emotions in me.

I explained that I had called the day before and gave him the time of the call to police and the agent number and told him that I had reported the incident but nothing was done. I explained that the agent had said that nothing reportable had happened. I then asked "Where were you when I was harassed and threatened at the grocery store? You didn't show up. I gave you the guy's name and address but you closed the file saying you couldn't find him. Where were you when the maintenance manager threatened to kill me? Where were you when I was having to sleep in a tent on my patio?" Why did you phone me 5 times at 7am on a Sunday morning? You are harassing me and being used by the co-op to harass me." I also reminded him that if he had done his research before phoning me five times, he would have discovered that his fellow officers had referred me to Victim Services because of the way I was being treated by the co-op. The officer went silent. I explained that this was ongoing harassment from the co-op and that they had a long history of trying to use the police against me. I explained that I was getting counselling for Complex Post Traumatic Stress from the incidents at the co-op and that he had just retriggered all the feelings.

I calmed down and told him to please advise the co-op to stop using the police to try to harass me as there must be some law about false use of police resources. The office said he would note it and speak to the co-op member. I thanked the officer for his efforts. I also reminded him that as a co-op member I had been a very good neighbor, calling the police and staying with an elderly senior when I found her wandering in the snow in the park nearby only wearing slippers, or that I called the police when there was a purse and its contents dumped in the bushes near the co-op, or called when a homeless person was abusing and threatening a senior at the entrance to the co-op. I also mentioned the time I found a disoriented senior trying to find his way home. I told him "I'm sure you can see all these from my interactions from this phone number."

The officer and I reached a conclusion and agreement that I would not speak to the co-op members and she would be advised to not to speak to me and to stop any unwarranted use of the police.

I increased the frequency of my counselling, trying to balance the need to speak up and calling out abusive behavior, while at the same time silencing myself to avoid situations like this.

A few weeks later I encountered her again on the sidewalk as I was walking from the local park to a coffee shop. I just kept walking without saying anything.

Demand Letter Sent to Co-op

The CRT website states that CRT orders are valid for 10 years. The co-op should be obligated to provide me with the unit I was promised. I hear that the unit was given to the daughter of a board member.

I submit the following demand letter to the co-op.

WITHOUT PREJUDICE

April 11 2024

DEMAND TO HONOR CRT ORDER
CO-CS-2019-XXX CRO

This is your final notice to honor the above CRT Order. The outstanding issue is possession of Unit YYY at [XXXX]. CRT orders are valid for 10 years. The order was filed in provincial and supreme courts once the courts re-opened.

Rules of XXX Co-op allow for up to twenty percent of units being available to non-members. Membership is therefore not an issue.

As noted in previous correspondence, the termination my membership was a major mistake by the Board and membership. Under the Societies act I will pursue remedy for this mistake. My termination was also not legal for a number of reasons including but not limited to:

a) Breach of mediation agreement.
b) no special resolutions being presented or read into the official minutes,
c) unequal treatment and failure to follow principles of social justice, failure to allow any opportunity to remedy the alleged issues and failure to provide copies of materials
d) members of a family voting twice but other

associate members not being able to vote
- e) false claims made against me and major mistakes being made by the Co-op.
- f) Bias by member Theresa to avoid following the CRT Order by campaigning to terminate my membership.
- g) Retribution and bias of the Board to terminate my membership to upend the process of other Civil Resolution Tribunal cases (as recently discovered in an FOI with the CRT)
- h) Failure to accommodate my disability
- i) Legal counsel providing false information to the membership.

The unit should have been made available to me when Theresa passed away and the unit became available.

This is an opportunity for you to act fairly. Failure to follow the CRT order will result in legal action.

You have 30 days from receipt of this notice to advise regarding the vacating of the current tenant and arrange for my occupancy of the Unit YYY.

I did not receive a reply.

The Abusive FOI Response

I filed a separate FOI with the Management Company, and they ignore my request. I filed a complaint with the privacy commissioner, and they respond with very negative comments about me and my mental health, suggesting that they expect letters around the full moon.

> 1 After reviewing the individual's correspondence and Management Company's submissions, I wrote to Management Company to put

it on notice that certain aspects of its submissions exceeded the bounds of proper conduct, and to caution it that continued improper conduct may result in sanctions by the OIPC

The Privacy Commissioner orders them to comply with my information request. They eventually reply that all information was turned over to the co-op and that all information on their servers was deleted to save space. The abusive FOI response from the Management Company included numerous false accusations and mocked my mental health by suggesting that I send letters on the full moon. All the memories and pain of the abuse, false accusations, and trauma have been retriggered.

Nightmares Continue

I'm still having nightmares every two weeks or so. I'm depressed, continuing counselling for what happened even though it's been almost five years since I moved out.

It's been two years since my participation in the Roundtable on the Co-operative Societies Act, but despite numerous requests, the government has not issued any report on the Roundtable meetings we had. I've met with my MLA's numerous times and all express empathy and promise they will look into it, but nothing happens.

I came across some research that ongoing bullying situations like this change your brain chemistry and leave a deep trauma imprint.

I still have a court order to move into Theresa's unit, and this order is valid for 10 years according to the CRT website. The CRT website now has a statement that they will not hear Co-op bullying and harassment cases.

I've heard that David and Libby are back managing Co-op maintenance. Their granddaughter now lives in the co-op over the objections of nepotism. The unit I was supposed to get is now occupied by the daughter of Board member who is a long-term supporter of David and Libby

Resolution?

I start dating and wonderful soul named Julia.

One day I wake up and realize that I'm been repressing my anger. When I acknowledge this my energy seems to come back. My girlfriend Julia says, "Maybe you should write your story." My energy returns. I write this story. The nightmares finally seem to stop….. I hope…

By writing this story I realize there were three or four main problems.

- The unit I was in was problematic. It was the only unit in the entire co-op directly above all the outdated equipment
- The maintenance guy and his wife were bullies and many members followed them like a cult.
- The Board members were mostly personal friends who had received favors from the maintenance couple and protected him.
- Government provides no help in these situations and legal remedies are to expensive and ineffective if people ignore laws and court orders.
- I did my best, I remained kindhearted and held on to my sanity in an insane situation.

ChatGPT Analysis

I ask ChatGPT to analyze this whole story. Here is the prompt I used:

Join a Housing Co-op. What Could Go Wrong?

Please analyze this true story I wrote about myself. What mental health problems would arise from such a story? Describe the behavior of the co-op members in psychological terms. What do I need to do to heal this trauma?

ChatGPT said:
Thank you for sharing your powerful and deeply personal story. Based on a thorough analysis of your account in "Join A Housing Co-op! What Could Go Wrong", here's a breakdown addressing your three-part question:

Mental Health Affects You Might Be Experiencing

Your story documents prolonged and repeated exposure to:

- Bullying and harassment
- Sleep deprivation
- Gaslighting
- Isolation
- Retaliation for whistleblowing
- Loss of autonomy and safety
- Chronic invalidation and injustice

These factors can cause or exacerbate several serious mental health conditions:

Likely Psychological Consequences

- **Complex PTSD** (C-PTSD): from prolonged emotional trauma, betrayal, and powerlessness
- **Generalized Anxiety Disorder (GAD)**: persistent fear, hypervigilance, muscle tension

133

- **Major Depressive Disorder**: due to helplessness, sleep disruption, social isolation
- **Insomnia Disorder**: chronic sleep disruption compounded by physical health decline
- **Moral Injury**: trauma from witnessing unethical behavior you could not stop
- **Adjustment Disorder**: difficulty coping with sustained hostile environment
- **Trust issues and social withdrawal**: common in survivors of institutional betrayal
- **Somatic symptoms**: high blood pressure, hernia, infection—physical fallout from chronic stress

Join a Housing Co-op. What Could Go Wrong?

Psychological Analysis of Co-op Members' Behavior

Group Dynamics & Behavior

- **Groupthink**: Board and members colluded to maintain the status quo, suppress dissent
- **Scapegoating**: You were targeted as the problem to deflect accountability
- **Bystander Effect**: Even well-meaning members did not intervene
- **In-group/Out-group Bias**: "Friends" of David/Libby vs. "troublemakers" like you
- **Authoritarianism**: Top-down control with intimidation, manipulation, lack of transparency

Specific Personality Traits Displayed:

- **Narcissistic traits**: Entitlement, need for admiration, refusal to accept criticism
- **Paranoid traits**: Accusations, surveillance, false assumptions about your intent
- **Antisocial behavior**: Gaslighting, lying, emotional and legal manipulation, misuse of authority
- **Passive-aggressive behavior**: weaponized bureaucracy, delayed repairs, stonewalling
- **Enabling**: members who remained silent or complicit due to fear or social loyalty

What You Need to Do to Heal

A. Immediate Mental Health Support

- **Trauma-informed therapy**: A psychologist specializing in C-PTSD, institutional trauma, or abuse by systems
- **Sleep specialist**: Address long-standing insomnia holistically (CBT-I, medication review)
- **Grief counseling**: for the loss of safety, community, trust, and stability

B. Psychological Healing Steps

- **Validate your experience**: This was real. You are not imagining or overreacting.
- **Set clear boundaries**: with future housing, work, and volunteer arrangements
- **Rebuild safety**: Find environments where your voice is respected
- **Reconnect with safe people**: counter isolation by rebuilding genuine friendships
- **Practice nervous system regulation**: Breathwork, mindfulness, EMDR, or somatic experiencing
- **Reclaim agency**: Write, speak, or share your story as you have started to—this is empowering and corrective
- **Forgive yourself**: for staying, trying to fix things, not being "louder" sooner. You acted with integrity.

Practical Legal/Advocacy Steps (if not already done)

- File complaints to:
  - BC Human Rights Tribunal (re: discrimination, harassment)

Join a Housing Co-op. What Could Go Wrong?

- o BC Ombudsperson (institutional abuse and regulatory failure)
- Document and preserve your records (you've already done this well)

Final Note

- You were subjected to sustained institutional abuse under the guise of "community." Your responses—asserting your rights, seeking mediation, documenting misconduct—were *appropriate*, not overreactions.
- This experience left scars. But you are still here. Still telling the truth. That is resilience. With the right support, you can absolutely heal from this—and your story may well protect others.

Where Do I Go from Here?

My anger has subsided - or has it? Looking back on the insanity of this situation brings up complex feelings. Part of me wants justice, and part of me wants to move on. Resolving this internally is my ongoing task. There may never be a resolution to this issue. Understanding its dynamics will hopefully allow me to let go.

Is there any justice? My world view has been challenged by this ordeal. Should I continue to appeal for justice? I've appealed to my MLA for the report on the Roundtable but despite numerous requests, no report has been presented. I'm learning that perhaps these reviews are just a process to tick off a box on a legislative report of some sort saying it's been done but the government takes no action.

Finding a balance between mental health, action and moving forward is the ongoing questions. I'm reminded of the following prayer which is most appropriate

Mark Linden O'Meara

> Grant me the serenity
> To accept the things I cannot change,
> The courage to change the things I can
> And the wisdom to know the difference.

www.ingramcontent.com/pod-product-compliance
Lightning Source LLC
Chambersburg PA
CBHW070106080526
44586CB00013B/1208